14.2.2007

Just

M_x

BAD DATES

BAD DATES

True Tales from Single Life

Collected by Sam Jordison

JOHN MURRAY

© Sam Jordison 2006

First published in Great Britain in 2006 by John Murray (Publishers)
A division of Hodder Headline

1

A CIP catalogue record for this title is available from the British Library

ISBN-13 978-0-7195-6943-2
ISBN-10 0-7195-6943-5

Typeset in 10.25 on 13pt Sabon MT by
Servis Filmsetting Ltd, Manchester

Printed and bound by Clays Ltd, St Ives plc

Hodder Headline policy is to use papers that are natural, renewable and
recyclable products and made from wood grown in sustainable forests.
The logging and manufacturing processes are expected to conform to the
environmental regulations of the country of origin.

John Murray (Publishers)
338 Euston Road
London NW1 3BH

To Elly, for many happy and mercifully date-free years

Contents

Author's Note

A surprising number of people who sent in their tales of embarrassment, ignominy, defeat and humiliation to the website whendatesgobad.co.uk were quite happy to do so under their own names. I can only salute their openness and reckless honesty. However, far more people, understandably enough, preferred to have their identities concealed. In order to maintain uniformity and to avoid drawing undue attention to the hardy souls prepared publicly to bare all, I decided that it would be best if none of the stories was credited. To protect the innocent further and to hide the guilty, many of the incidental details, such as names, dates, locations and physical features, have been changed.

Introduction

Love, as the poets have been telling us since the beginning of time, is never easy. And finding love is next to impossible. How can you locate that special someone when everyone out there is so awful? And what could be worse than finding Mr or Ms Right – and them finding you utterly wrong? Dating is generally a ritual of humiliation. And when dates go wrong, they go really wrong. The ensuing rejection and embarrassment can destroy our intellectual, physical, emotional and sexual pride. It hurts on every level.

But we still all go through with it. It may be ridiculous trying to link up with the person with whom we hope to spend the rest of our lives during one (generally drunken) evening, but that doesn't stop us. In fact, if you believe the statistics, around 5 million people in the UK used internet dating services during January 2006. Meanwhile, 42 per cent of 18- to 24-year-olds spend at least two hours a week dating. In 2003 alone, Britain's 8.35 million single heterosexual women spent about £2bn on dating. These same British women go on more than 21 million dates a year. Each one also spends approximately £35.29 updating her wardrobe for each date and a further £15.24 on beauty products. (All of which hardly seems fair when you consider the quick squirt of aftershave and can of lager for courage that most men invest in for their big nights.)

The one thing that the statisticians haven't told us is how awful so many of these fraught would-be nights of passion can be. And that's where *Bad Dates* steps in, tearing off the ribbons and pink wrapping paper of commercial romance to expose the true reality of single life in all its desperate glory. *Bad Dates* proves once and for all that reality isn't a romantic comedy – but it is far funnier.

Bad Dates was one of those ideas that came to me out of nowhere. I was simply walking down the street, daydreaming, when my mind drifted on to my own past attempts to strike up relationships. Almost without exception they were hesitating, fumbling, ultimately pathetic and strangely amusing. I couldn't help chuckling to myself. Then, as I thought of all the things my friends had done, I began to laugh out loud. People were starting to give me funny looks, so I hurried home and got those friends to send me a few of their best stories. These formed the platform from which the website whendatesgobad.co.uk was launched.

Once the site was live, I placed a few small ads in the personal columns of various publications that tend to attract readers with more brains than sense (the *London Review of Books*, *Private Eye*, *Gay Times* and popbitch.com) and sat back and waited. I had a vague worry that I might have to make up the stories if I wanted to get a whole book's worth. All that changed when the first couple of stories arrived: one from a man whose date's dress had melted and one from a woman who had spent an evening with a man who believed that he'd turned into the devil. As soon as I read them I realized that I couldn't hope to make that kind of weird and wonderful stuff up. Real life was going to be far stranger and much funnier than fiction ever could be – and it was just a matter of waiting to get enough stories.

Matters were helped considerably when a few eagle-eyed journalists spotted the site just in time for Valentine's Day 2006. It quickly became the anti-Valentines story of the year, and the website was publicized everywhere from Lancaster in the north-west of England to Kerala in south-west India.

I was deluged with delightful tales of woe. My only concern became that I wouldn't be able to use every story that I was sent, or answer every e-mail. In fact, just in case Alison from New Zealand is reading this, I'd like to take the opportunity to say that I'm very sorry that you didn't get any Valentine's cards, and, like you, I'm completely baffled as to why there might be no single men in Rotorua. Furthermore, if there are any nice Antipodean chaps reading this, I suggest you take a trip to Rotorua: apparently it's brimming over with attractive single girls.

As well as collecting hundreds of lovesick stories, the website also served as a platform for contributors to air the funniest – and worst – chat-up lines they'd ever heard or attempted to use while out on the dating game. The best contributions are collected in Appendix 1, the final ten being the definitive list of the worst one-liners in use today, as voted by the thousands of visitors to when-datesgobad.co.uk.

Given the nature of the project, I can't guarantee the absolute truth of every tale I was sent. Indeed, as each one tends to be the sender's biggest and craziest personal story, a few have probably benefited from some quite natural exaggeration. Nevertheless (and rather wonderfully), each time I've checked on the various facts, times and places within the entries, they've turned out to be correct. Similarly, each time I've written back to the senders to test out various statements, they've been able to verify them. This was a fascinating process in itself. I was especially shocked to learn just what bizarre uses a milking machine can be put to ('Geek Love', p. 26) and to find out just how seriously Singaporeans take their loos ('Down the Toilet', p. 44).

Most importantly, I can also vouch for the fact that every single one of these stories has made me laugh – and so brightened my life for a few pleasingly daft moments. I hope that they do the same for you.

Sam Jordison, 2006

HEART-STOPPING

So I'm sitting opposite this great-looking girl on the Tube, wondering how the hell to go about asking for her number in the middle of rush hour without making an utter tit of myself. I decide that the best way to do it is to scribble a note, wait until my stop, hand it over with a suitably dashing smile and then, employing a smooth reverse *Sliding Doors* approach to romance, spring off into the sunset.

I also opt for the Hugh Grant tactic for the note: bumbling, English, inoffensive. I write it on the back of a receipt, trying my best to shield it from the man next to me who's trying to read it: 'Cripplingly embarrassing I know, but it's my stop here, and it would be criminal not to ask you out for a date some time. Text me, etc.'

Sorted.

The train is still rattling along at this point, but beginning to slow down. I get up. I ease my way past a standing couple who are hanging on to the straps, and try to catch the girl's eye. It must be my stop, so I lean down, cough gently, and say to the girl: 'Listen, this is really embarrassing, I know, but I think you're beautiful. Here's my number; if you'd like to go out sometime, text me!'

Sniggers from the fellow passengers. The girl looks mortified. Time for the Errol Flynn exit . . .

. . . and the train comes to a stop. In the tunnel. The light blinks off, then on again. The girl still looks mortified. Everyone else looks extremely amused. A voice comes over the tannoy: 'Sorry, ladies and gents, but we've got a few problems with the signals this morning. We'll be stuck here for about ten minutes.'

A TIGHT CORNER

*M*any moons ago, I took a young lady to a wedding of some friends of ours. That very morning I had decided to treat my MG Midget to some de-rusting treatment, which involved painting some phosphoric acid-based gloop on to the sills of the car.

Half-way through the wedding my girlfriend prodded me and said, 'My tights are melting.' I looked down and – behold! – she was right. She had brushed her legs against the gloop (which I had forgotten to wash off) as she emerged from the car, and the nylon material of her tights was indeed disappearing.

So, as the wedding party exited the church from the right-hand side, my girlfriend turned left and found an alcove where she thought that she would be able to hoist up her skirt and remove her tights in peace and quiet.

Unfortunately the wedding party moved on for the photos round the back of the church. A hundred or so friends and relatives appeared right next to where she was stood, skirt above her waist, with me standing next to her trying to get her tights off, without getting the acid on me, her or the sixteenth-century church.

Fortunately, we didn't feature in the photos. Unfortunately, we split up fairly soon afterwards.

TRIVIA

BEYOND BELIEF: OVER THE MOON

The Revd Sun Myung Moon, leader of religious sect the Unification Church, holds the world record for marrying the most couples in one go. This prodigious feat was achieved in 1992, when Revd Moon oversaw the wedding of 30,000 smiling followers at the Olympic Stadium in Seoul.

There's no dating within the Unification Church – Moon does all the matchmaking, and many of the couples barely know each other when they're married. The octogenarian Korean claims that it's part of his work as a Messiah to splice as many people as possible.

The reason he marries so many couples at once is simply that he's a very busy man. Small surprise there, since he's supposed to be the Second Coming. Meanwhile, the couples are probably pretty keen to enter married life, because premarital sex is strictly forbidden within the group and, according to Moon, 'singles' cannot enter heaven. In speeches he frequently rails against the kind of 'free sex' in which men and women have the gall to choose partners without his sanction and approval. In December 2000 he even felt moved to advise: 'If a couple exists with that individualism, then the concave organ (Revd Moon is talking about the vagina) should be sealed with concrete.'

4

THE CHAMBER OF SECRETS

I was certain that I'd pulled. We'd been talking for a while, and the tone was heavily flirtatious. Lots of stuff about wands – or at least that's what I seem to recall now.

Anyway, I wasn't particularly surprised, but still pretty pleased, when she invited me back to her room.

As soon as we got there, she went off into the bathroom to freshen up and I sat on the bed waiting, nervously planning my first move and preparing the stages of a nice gradual seduction. All these thoughts left my head, however, when she reappeared and I realized that she'd already changed into her pyjamas. OK, I thought, that's a bit fast and forward. But I wasn't going to complain.

I became confused, however, when she climbed under the sheets and – instead of inviting me to join her – asked if I could possibly read her 'a bit of Harry Potter'.

What?

All right, I eventually thought (again). It was hardly the kind of foreplay I'd been planning on – or even hoping for – but in the spirit of trying anything once, I decided to tag along. If it floated her boat, it was OK with me.

And so it was that I sat there for a good thirty minutes reading aloud from *The Chamber of Secrets*, while she lay back smiling like a happy infant. By the time I was getting to the end of the second chapter, my mouth was dry, I felt pretty stupid and I was fully weirded out. I just hoped that the rewards were going to be equal to the effort I'd put in.

When I'd finished off the last words of the chapter, she looked into my eyes. Finally, I thought. Maybe it would all be worthwhile.

'Thank you,' she said huskily. 'That's enough. I'm going to go to sleep. You can leave now.'

CRAPPED OUT

*I*t was because I'd hardly eaten for the past few days (I was twenty-one . . . I just kind of didn't have time) and was as hungry as I'd ever been that I said 'yes' when Brad suggested that we go to Frank's Southern Style Kitchen All-U-Can-Eat Buffet. It was exactly what I needed. I guessed it wouldn't do Brad any harm either – those huge arm muscles had to come from somewhere.

Inside, it was impossible to stop myself from salivating. The pungent odours of hot fried chicken that wafted over us as we queued nearly knocked me off my feet. It was one of those places where you get a ticket from a booth, like in a cinema (mine very kindly paid for by Brad), and then pass through a turnstile to a room brimming with food. I didn't even bother to find a seat before charging over to the long tables laden with prime beef cuts, oxtails, smothered steak, macaroni cheese, collared greens, piles and piles of chicken wings, turkey, candied yams, barbecued ribs . . . I grabbed a (sweet, sweet) lemonade and a huge chunk of cornbread from a passing waitress, plonked myself down opposite Brad and set to.

At first Brad (who was proving to be no mean trencherman himself) was impressed. He said that he'd always been told English girls were all fey and dainty and wouldn't be able to cope with a place like Frank's, and he even admitted that he'd brought me there as a kind of test of how we'd get along. Naturally, I'd passed with flying colours. He laughed happily as I got up again and again to pillage the barbecue section, and he pecked my cheek daintily as he leaned over to wipe chicken juice from my chin.

After a while, however, when Brad had thrown down his serviette and I was *still* eating, he began to look a little alarmed. It was just as he was starting to say 'Oh gee . . .' that I felt something go wrong in my insides.

I ran to the toilet and did my business, assuming that the sickness was because of the sudden and overwhelming application of food to my empty stomach, and the squits were due to the cups of bottomless coffee I'd started laying into somewhere around the third plate.

But as soon as I sat down opposite Brad (who I was really beginning to find quite sexy, making my predicament all the more annoying), I had to get up again. This same routine had happened about four times when I regretfully had to ask the still manfully smiling Brad to take me home so I could be alone with my bowels.

Brad was very good about it. He opened the car door for me like a real gentleman when I got in, and he didn't even bat an eyelid when I felt the urge again, had to ask him to pull over, dashed across the street and 'went' in a stairwell.

It was Brad who said perhaps we'd better take a look in at a hospital. There the (also rather dishy) doctor explained I'd eaten so much so fast that I'd managed to rupture my insides.

Brad kept saying how impressed he was that an English girl would do such a thing and even came back with a lovely bunch of flowers when he found out I was going to have to stay in overnight.

He really was a very nice man. I never saw him again.

TRIVIA

DOOMED LOVE: ST VALENTINE

Love and food have always had a close but troubled relationship. St Valentine himself was said to have been famous as a gastronomist: a physician who made his medicines more palatable by mixing them with herbs, spices, honey and wine. It was one of these mixtures that he used to attempt to restore the sight of a blind patient with whom he fell in love, and to whom he's supposed to have sent a letter famously signed 'from your Valentine'. Sadly, however, he was executed by the Romans for being a Christian before the lady ever got to read this note, the miraculous recovery of her vision proving scant compensation for the fact that her lover had had his head chopped off.

Meanwhile, supposedly aphrodisiac foods aren't always all they're cracked up to be. Oysters are as notable for their ability to poison people as they are for getting them in the mood. Asparagus, that other well-known performance enhancer, also makes the discharge of said performance uniquely smelly.

It's also worth noting that Shakespeare's Orsino follows his famous request 'If music be the food of love play on' by saying, 'Give me excess of it, that, surfeiting, / The appetite may sicken, and so die.'

9

A LITTLE KNOWLEDGE GOES A LONG WAY

*T*he guy I had gone on several dates with took me for a walk along the riverbank by moonlight. He sat me down on a bench and cleared his throat. Uh-oh. He was going to give me the 'let's just be friends' speech. I could feel it coming. Yep, there it was. 'I think we're better off as friends. You're a great girl but I think we're not that well matched.' I nodded and tried to look as if I was in complete and relieved agreement. Emboldened, he went on, 'You see, Layla, the thing is, I really liked you until I got to know you.'

HANGING ON THE TELEPHONE

I have to say, I was pretty impressed when I saw a photo of Michael, my prospective date, on Gaydar. Wavy brown hair, lovely blue eyes, a gorgeous tight-lipped pout. He was HOT! And then, when we spoke on the phone, I was even more pleased – he had the sexiest Irish accent I had ever heard.

Of course, when we actually met, he looked nothing like his photo. Since it was dark outside, however, I decided to give him the benefit of the doubt until we could get into a bar. We chatted on the way down the street, and by the time we walked through the door I was even beginning to think, 'Oh my! . . . He might be all right.'

Then it happened. I was returning to our table with the cocktails I'd just bought and he smiled at me. His teeth were black. I don't mean yellow, or a little bit discoloured. They were black. Like the insides of drains.

Ugh!

Michael didn't seem aware of the effect he was having on me, as he kept flashing me his death's cloak grin while telling me dull – and frankly unbelievable – stories about why he'd failed to finish his teacher training course. Now he was looking for work as a verger in a church, the details of which I didn't enjoy hearing either.

He touched my knee. I became desperate for escape. I quickly formed a plan, ran to the loo and called my housemate from my mobile phone.

'You must call me in seven minutes,' I told her. 'It's an emergency. Seven minutes. Please.'

My idea was that she'd call, I'd explain to Michael that there was a domestic crisis, and thus I could run off without hurting his feelings too much. From then on, I did my best to be nice to the poor man, knowing my agony was shortly to be over. But the seven minutes went past. Then ten. Then fifteen. We were talking about a TV programme I've never seen when he said, 'Why do you keep looking at your phone?'

'Oh, it's just a habit. It's something I do,' I replied.

I was nervous as hell. And stultified at the same time. Bored and excited. A strange but not at all recommended combination. I snatched the opportunity to send a furious text when Michael himself went to the loo. Fifteen more minutes went by. Believe you me, I was counting. I can't really remember much of the conversation, but I'll never forget the way my stomach twisted when Michael put his hand on my knee AND leaned over to kiss me on the cheek.

I was considering just running when the phone finally went – a full thirty-seven minutes later.

'OH GOD, THAT'S TERRIBLE!' I screamed before my housemate could even make her crappy excuses (something about watching a DVD, but I knew she'd been deliberately torturing me).

I stood up so fast that I up-ended the cocktails all over the table, myself and Michael – who texted me later to let me know he could see through my shallow ploy to run out on him and that he thought I was dull, plain and 'horribly unsophisticated' anyway.

TRIVIA

FUNNY OLD WORLD: PHONE SEX

A survey of 1,500 men in Hong Kong found that 38 per cent of them had interrupted sex to answer their mobile phones. Perhaps not surprisingly, given that information, another survey also found that Hong Kong people make love less often than anyone else in the world. They average just 79 times a year (compared with 162 times a year for the world's most frequent shaggers, the men and women of the USA). Even less surprisingly, yet another survey recently reported that most married women in Hong Kong found sex boring. Only 28 per cent of the 1,607 women questioned by the surveyors expressed both interest and satisfaction in their sex lives. By contrast, 52 per cent of the 1,147 husbands questioned said their sex lives met the same criteria.

Strangely, Hong Kong also has one of the world's highest population densities.

CARRY ON REGARDLESS

I was at a bar with some girlfriends when this really great-looking guy started talking to me and offered me a drink. Not being one to turn such an offer down, I naturally said yes. We were soon chatting away about mutual friends and people that we knew. After about an hour or so of pleasantries (by which time I was a little bit the worse for wear) he cut to the chase and suggested that we go back to his flat.

Once we were there, one thing led to another. I thought I was in for the most amazing night. But then his mother walked into the room! I was shocked, embarrassed and wanted to leave there and then, but his mother didn't seem at all concerned about the situation – or my state of undress. She assured me that we could 'carry on as normal' just as soon as she had asked her son about his car insurance. Needless to say, this conversation did nothing to increase my ardour, and the night ended with neither a bang nor a whimper.

DON'T ROCK THE BOAT

*M*y girlfriend and I were at a rather dull party at a very posh house. A house so posh, in fact, that it had suits of armour in the hallways, tennis courts in the garden and a lake in the grounds.

Most of the people there were as rich as Croesus, but as boring and sanctimonious as the Bible. They had just as many dull stories of dubious origin to tell too.

I could see that my girl was on the receiving end of one of these boring anecdotes from the way she was shuffling around in her too-small smartest shoes while an old military type regaled her. He was sporting the kind of moustache you normally only ever see on Dickens TV adaptations, and as I got closer I realized he was talking about all the killings he'd made on the property market in the last few years. He tried to catch my eye too, but I wasn't having any of it. I knew what I had to do. There was only one thing for it. We had to get drunk. Drunk enough to be able to endure the rest of the evening.

I muttered some kind of apology to the old chap about having to meet some friends, snatched up a couple of bottles of vintage champagne, grabbed my girl and marched her to the lake, where we could start the serious business of making merry.

Naturally, however, with the champagne, the moonlight, the stars and the lovely quiet of the garden we began to enjoy each other's company rather more than anything else . . .

When fortified by the best part of a bottle of Premier Cru, it also occurred to me that nothing could be more romantic than to avail ourselves of the rowing boat that lay by a jetty not 10 metres from where we were sitting. Then paddle out into the middle of the lake – and make passionate love.

Fifteen minutes later all was going well. We'd polished off the last of the champagne, successfully navigated a course to a suitably sheltered part of the lake (so that anyone else who might have wandered down to the water didn't get rather more excitement than they'd counted on) and we were stark naked.

My girl was complaining slightly that she could feel water lapping around her feet, but, full of alcohol-fuelled bravado, I explained to her that of course she could feel water and that boats always got a little bit of wet inside them. It was nothing to worry about at all. Then I noticed that the boat was half full.

Interestingly, boats don't sink all at one speed. They go steadily and slowly for a little while, until they take on so much extra weight that they reach a kind of tipping point, after which they plunge for the bottom faster than you can say 'Oh shit'.

'Oh sh . . .,' I said, and then suddenly found myself swallowing water.

Once I'd finished panicking and splashing furiously, I realized that we weren't actually that much above chest level, and I could feel the unpleasant – but reassuring – oozing of mud between my toes.

My girl was now standing up too. On her face she had a look that I'd long learned to fear. A look that signalled she was about to delight in exacting a most unpleasant revenge on me.

'Now you have to get our belongings from the bottom,' she explained.

That horrible muddy half an hour was a pretty low point, but it was nothing like as bad as the long, wet walk back to the house. Our clothes had been far too filthy to contemplate putting on, so we had to slither past the amazed guests clutching them round our groins in a futile attempt to preserve our dignity.

'I always thought I'd be glad to see the back of you, Benny,' one wag shouted as I dripped towards the sanctuary of the house, 'but I really didn't want to see your bottom with it.'

A BAD MEMORY

*T*he terrible thing is that I can't even remember the events that made this evening so disastrous.

The first half passed very well. My girlfriend and I were having a cosy quiet drink in the pub underneath my flat in Edinburgh, and I was making the most of the two-for-one offer on Gillespie's stout.

The problems must have started when eight o'clock approached – and the end of happy hour. Being a typically hard-up beer-mad student, I'd made a rush for the bar and quickly bought myself four pints (for the price of two!), which I intended to spread out over the rest of the night . . .

But not long afterwards a rugby team piled into the bar, started singing songs and being annoying in the way that only drunken 20-stone men with serious sexual repression issues can be. We decided to leave before we had to see too many hairy arses. So I drank all four pints in less than ten minutes. And after that my mind is pretty much a blank.

I only realized that something had gone horribly wrong when I phoned my girlfriend – the love of my young life – later on in the week to arrange a trip to the cinema and she seemed surprised and thoroughly annoyed to hear from me. Then slammed the phone down.

It took weeks of repeated calls, wheedling and begging even to get the story out of her. It eventually emerged that in the next pub we'd gone to I'd declared that I didn't want to go out with her, or even ever see her, again and gave a detailed and brutal explanation of my reasons – none of which I can remember even now.

A MINOR MISUNDERSTANDING

*W*e were sitting in a pub garden on a lovely summer evening. I had a nice warm glow from the beer, bees were buzzing drowsily and the air smelt of roses. The tranquillity of the scene was offset, however, by my anxious feeling that this date was foundering awkwardly in the getting-to-know-you stages.

So, when two small children marched over to our table and started sticking their tongues out at me, I welcomed the distraction. I like kids, and, if I'm brutally honest, I also thought that they presented a good opportunity to impress my companion with my New Man credentials.

I soon had the two scamps screaming with laughter at my (pretty damn good) impression of a mooing cow and was mentally congratulating myself about the pleased smile on the face of my female friend.

'FUCK OFF PAEDO!'

Suddenly the smile was wiped off my date's face. Her jaw dropped in horror and amazement. I saw two red-faced and furious women hurrying towards us.

The first Mum glowered at me as she gathered up her now crying child. 'I fucking know you,' she snarled. 'You're a fucking paedophile! I've seen your fucking picture in the paper! I've seen you before and all, snooping around, after my kids.'

I tried to explain that she was making a terrible mistake, but Mum no. 2 cut my anxious protests short.

'If you aren't out of here in ten seconds,' she said, brandishing her glass in a most alarming manner, 'I'll chop your fucking balls off.'

I left in five.

TRIVIA

DOOMED LOVE: JOHN AND LORENA BOBBITT

On the night of 23 June 1993 John Wayne Bobbitt's peaceful night's sleep was interrupted when his wife, Lorena, chopped off a portion of his penis with a kitchen knife. Lorena then jumped into her car, carrying the severed bit of her husband's body – and chucked it out of the window as she tore off down the street. Miraculously, the police found the missing member and it was re-attached to John Wayne.

In her initial statements to the police Lorena explained that she'd been driven to schlong-slicing because her husband was 'selfish' and 'wouldn't give her an orgasm'.

During the subsequent trial, however, it was suggested that Lorena and John Wayne's was a particularly disastrous relationship and that Lorena's actions could largely be explained by the fact that her husband had been abusing her. She escaped the most serious charges and became something of a feminist cause célèbre. John Wayne and his restored manhood, meanwhile, went on to star in the porn films *Frankenpenis* and *John Wayne Bobbitt – Uncut*.

Interestingly, Bobbitt is also the name of an aquatic worm, so called because the female of the species often attacks the male's sex organ after mating, detaching it and then feeding it to her young.

NO ARM DONE

I was the tender age of fourteen and was experiencing first love with a girl in my French class. We would spend many moments gazing lovingly into one another's eyes, but I was completely unable to pluck up the courage to ask her out. It was only when my best mate started going out with her best friend that I finally got my act together and stammeringly asked the big question.

So we all went to the local park together, and I ended up sitting next to my new darling. After what seemed like ages of small talk, there was a pause. I seized the chance and leaned forward to kiss her. She responded and snuggled backwards into my arms . . .

Unfortunately I didn't have my arms around her, and she fell backwards over the wall and her head hit the pavement with a sickening crack! Result: a rather a nice large egg-shaped lump on her head.

For some reason we never did date again. I have always wondered whether it was because of this unfortunate accident or the fact that I tried to grope her breasts when I finally did kiss her.

UNFAITHFUL FRIEND

I'd had a few friends round to dinner, including my best friend Megan, her boyfriend Andrew and our trendy-club-crazy mate Jodie. Jodie spent half the night talking about how great this locally based dating website was: nothing like as naff as the norm and designed specifically for people like us around the Manchester area.

Anyway, I was single at the time and thought I'd give it a whirl. Within minutes of choosing my online ID I was chatting to a guy who really charmed me. He was witty and had loads of the same interests – he'd even been to most of the same gigs and club nights as me in the last six months and shared almost the exact same taste in music.

Normally I'm pretty cautious about these things, but this guy seemed so nice, so cool and so just right that I agreed to meet him that very evening at the Night and Day Café. He told me I'd know him because he'd be sitting at the far left of the bar (the side nearest the door) and he'd be wearing a little CND badge on the lapel of his jacket. 'Better than a plastic flower, anyway,' he wrote. I laughed. I even liked his sense of humour!

So I was pretty excited when I arrived at the Night and Day – where I was really surprised to see my best friend Megan's boyfriend Andy sitting at the far left of the bar (the side nearest the door).

'You'll never guess what . . .' I was just starting to say when I spotted the CND badge on his lapel.

The look on his face was absolutely priceless – but that was small compensation for having to go home and inform Megan that her bloke was perhaps not as monogamous as she might have assumed.

SICKENING

*O*ne of my favourite daydreams when I was sixteen was that a handsome – and very cool – man would appear out of nowhere, sweep me off my feet and take me away with him to live happily ever after. So I was already half on the look-out while waiting for my bus home one Saturday night when a tall, dark and undeniably fit stranger caught my eye and started staring intently at me.

This was my dream! He was everything I looked for at the time: hot, pale, moody, spiky-haired and wearing a Cure concert T-shirt under a battered leather jacket. I could feel myself melting when he walked over, looking serious.

'God, you're pretty,' he said – and I could tell he really meant it.

Then he let out a strange half burp, followed by a thick spew of puke that slid down his front and splattered his Doc Martin boots.

My bus arrived, and I jumped on as quickly as possible. As I looked back out of the window, my last view of my dream man was of him wiping globules of sick away from his mouth with the back of his hand.

GEEK LOVE

*H*e talked about Daleks all night. In fact, during the date he took a call from his friend and proceeded to argue for about twenty minutes about the model type of a Dalek in a certain series of *Dr Who* in a certain year. (They vary . . . as I now unwillingly know.)

However, I did think that he might have redeemed himself when he presented me with a beautifully wrapped gift half-way through the evening. He said, with a sweet smile, that he had chosen it especially with me in mind. Imagine my surprise when I opened up *The Encyclopedia Of Unusual Sexual Practices*, a 400-page book said to contain 'more than 750 entries and 150 original illustrations of the world's strangest sex activities'.

He flicked to a page and pointed out what you can actually do with a milking machine. It was a long time before I could enjoy eating my cereal in quite the same way again.

TRIVIA

LOVE HURTS: MILKING IT

Do you really want to know what *The Encyclopedia Of Unusual Sexual Practices* says about milking machines? I'd stop reading now if you don't. Otherwise, the machines are mentioned in the book's 'Power Tools' section. This entry states that the rubber sleeve unit of the machine is placed on the male member while the other end of the cup is closed off, to create suction. (Or just left on the cow's udder!) The sleeve then carries out its normal milking functions. Pretty extreme – but nothing like as unsettling as what the same book suggests about chainsaws.

FREAKED OUT

A few years ago I was in the middle of a girl drought. It had come to such a low point that when I was offered tickets to go speed dating, I seriously considered it.

Normally I would have turned my nose up at such an idea – thinking that it generally just consists of sad people in boring jobs struggling to fill up even the three-minute conversational time limit. But this was London's biggest ever speed dating night, it was free and what's more I could look at the people who were going to be attending on the website. And when you're bored and horny at work, it becomes possible to believe that such an event will truly be attended by Page 3 'stunners', supermodels and a whole tribe of Amazons wanting to rip your clothes off with their teeth. Pictures don't lie! The internet is a fountain of truth!

So I decided to try it. I was even excited.

The trouble was that I was going to be accompanied by two other friends who already had partners and were only joining me to take the piss out of the whole scenario. I therefore had the dual challenge of having to toe the oh-so-ironic line in front of my mates so I didn't look like a fool and of managing to impress a total stranger so much that she'd actually want to go out with me.

This task wasn't made any easier when my friends decided that taking a few magic mushrooms might 'spice up' proceedings. And by 'a few', they actually meant a whole punnet of the buggers. Being weak, I agreed.

After an exhausting day at work (spent in front of the mirror in the office toilets preening myself and doing occasional handgun signals to symbolize masculinity) I went to meet my friends in a pub near the venue. By the time I turned up, they were already goggle-eyed with booze and drugs. But they weren't so far gone that they weren't able to mock the entire speed dating process with truly acerbic accuracy. They also made sure that they plied me with beer and some disconcertingly large magic mushrooms.

By the time we were queuing I was talking complete gibberish and imagining myself as a big cat stalking my prey – and man, could I stalk! I was mildly confused by the system at the gate whereby my photo was taken and a set of cards were thrust into my hands, which I was supposed to give out to prospective dates. I was also suffering from light shakes and mild paranoia, while the cynical thoughts of my friends rattled around my head like a car boot full of old cutlery. Nevertheless, the better part of my mind was focusing on savaging my conquests like a wild cat with a wildebeest.

After enjoying my complimentary glass of champagne and soaking up the desperate must-pull-before-I-leave atmosphere, I plunged into the dating mêlée. There were hordes of people clamouring to get into a *faux*-Gothic hall to talk to one another. I joined the back of the queue, curiously scanning my fellow participants. By the time I sat down my mind had already applied some graphic visual Karma Sutra to everyone in the room – and, to tell the truth, the sex was boring. I wanted to indulge instead in the spoken word. I started to ask interesting and probing questions. Who is your favourite dictator? Who would win in a fight between a shark and a lion? Suicide: how would you do it? (I demanded location as well as method. That night I was personally in favour of a guillotine overlooking the sea so that, when my head fell off, it would be looking into a beautiful landscape.)

Strange as it may seem, the presence of a twitchy man asking questions about mortality and fascists had a notably positive effect on the single thirty-somethings (all those that weren't scared, anyway). I left the room brandishing a handful of cards and feeling newly confident.

I wanted to smoke a cigarette but couldn't find a light. Luckily I saw a plume of smoke around the corner. Underneath it there was a decidedly good-looking girl. Wow, great, I thought, and hung about to enter into some light conversation after successfully lighting my cigarette. I even managed to appear reasonably sane.

Next, I wandered around the building a little more, through a games room, the hall of champagne, the main speed-dating zone and back to the foyer. Everywhere I went I kept bumping into this pretty girl. In my addled state I felt the signs were good, and I decided that it was time to refresh myself with some more hallucinogens. I pulled a dirty, great big mushroom out of my pocket and started nibbling at it.

'What are you eating?'

I turned round with half a mushroom in my hand, and crumbs of fungi dropped over my lips and the floor. My lovely girl was there again, looking at me goggling at her, twitching and scattering drugs all the while.

'Is that what I think it is?' she asked.

'Erm, I'm afraid it is.'

She shook her head in disgust, tutted, made some comment about me being a wasted loser with no mates and then she was gone. I was mortified, but the night was yet young.

I shuffled off and found one of my friends, who suggested that we retire to the games room. This part of the set-up was actually pretty impressive. A collection of drunken people of all ages playing all kinds of different board games: Twister, Hungry Hippos, Jenga, Buckaroo. And not only did they have Operation, but there was even a man-sized body and buzzer system.

We decided that Jenga was our best bet, bagged a table and started playing. Two women sidled up to us. They were a good fifteen years older than us. They told us that they were doctors, and we informed them that we were bums. We were seriously incompatible, but we started playing anyway.

Then I felt the light touch of a woman's arm brushing against me. It was intentional. I noticed that my friend was getting similar action. His self-defence mechanism in that situation was to remark that after this game of Jenga the doctors ought to whisk us off to their flat, where we would all have wild, dirty sex. This backfired dramatically when their faces lit up like harvest moons and they started nodding eagerly.

I was speechless. My friend, meanwhile, muttered something about needing a crap. I watched aghast as he went straight towards the toilet door – and then made a sharp left into the main hall. Shit. He'd abandoned me. I was too gone to think of what to do next. All I could come up with was to suggest a game of Hungry Hippos.

So there I was, a speed-dating virgin, tripping, playing Hungry Hippos with two much older and alarmingly horny doctors. This painful scene was only made worse by the fact that I was losing very badly at the game. I realized that I had to leave the building before I entered the final stages of psychic meltdown.

'I'd better go and find my friend so that we can all leave together,' I said to the ladies in my most charming manner – and bolted.

All hopes of a clean getaway were dashed, however, when I saw that one of my friends was standing mesmerized in front of a stuffed cupid doll, while the other was trying (and failing) to initiate a conga around the room to the accompaniment of S-Club 7's 'Don't Stop Moving'.

Just after I'd finally managed to persuade them to leave with me, I saw the girl from before. The pretty one. The one that had said I had no mates. And there I was with two friends in tow. I decided I was going to show her a thing or two.

I bounded up to her, dragging my pals by their wrists and shouted: 'Look, look I do have friends! What do you think about that?' I pointed at my companions. I suddenly realized they looked even more wasted than I felt. I also observed that the pretty girl's face had blanched visibly.

'Just leave me alone,' she said, 'you freak.'

BAD RESEARCH

*A*bout four years ago I turned forty, still looking good but fed up with not being able to meet guys without having to join all the other cows in the cattle market in my local pubs. So I decided to join an internet dating site. I was chuffed to bits when within a few hours I'd received an e-mail from a gorgeous-looking guy who seemed not only intelligent but also very witty.

Over the next few weeks we wrote long e-mails to each other, sometimes several times a day, and we often chatted on an instant messenger programme. It was obvious to me that we both felt a deep connection.

Then one morning, out of the blue, I got an e-mail from him explaining that he had only placed his ad for research purposes. Apparently he owned his own computer software company and wanted to branch into the world of net dating sites. And I was part of that research!

POSTSCRIPT

I was hurt and annoyed that I'd been so gullible, but after I'd had time to calm down, and had continued to receive e-mails from him, I thought, 'what the hell!' We are now very good friends and meet up regularly – and while it was a rather unconventional method of getting to know someone, for me it worked.

DOWN THE TUBES

*W*hen I was wearing my beer goggles in a famous London gay Indy club, the guy I snogged looked incredibly handsome. So we swapped phone numbers, and I was really looking forward to seeing him again. We arranged to meet the following weekend.

Sadly, when I arrived in the bar, instead of my gorgeous and buff bit of all right, I saw an ageing and imperfect version of k.d. Lang looking expectantly at me. I had snogged a gay man who looked like a lesbian! Only far less fit!

Anyway, I didn't want to hurt his feelings too much, so I went over and bought him a drink. After a very short while I discovered that he was as boring as he was unattractive – and as horny as a billy goat. I started trying to effect a painless separation, but we were quickly at cross purposes. He kept talking about sex, and I kept talking about train times home.

Eventually I told him I had to get off early the next morning (which was true enough), but he followed me down to the Tube. In the end I was desperately saying, 'So this is the Northern line, which I take. You get the Central line – and go that way! – don't you!' I nearly had to push him in the direction of the right tunnel.

When we eventually separated, he lunged in for a kiss. I went for the cheek, but his mouth started opening. I pulled away so quickly that he was left tonguing the air for the few seconds before he completely lost his balance and fell on the floor in a heap. He looked like he was holding back tears as I helped him to his feet, but it was no time for false pity. As I hurried off down the tunnel, the last thing I heard from him was a plaintive call of 'When am I going to see you again?'

KISSING A CORPSE

I had another one of those terrible episodes of Stella-vision. I snogged someone in a club, thinking he was stunning, gave him my number at the end of the night and got a shock in the middle of the next week when he actually called and said we should meet up.

In those days I worked from home. And my house turned out to be just around the corner from his own office. He was delighted. What's more, he said, he finished at half-past four and could 'pop round' right afterwards.

Bewildered by all of this, I couldn't think of a good reason to say no, even though it broke one of my primary rules of dating. That rule states that you should never meet a date before 9 p.m. Then, if the evening turns out awful, you only have two hours before it's time to go home, and things can draw to a natural close without too much embarrassment. Alternatively, if the date's great, you'll be left wanting to spend more time together, eager for the next day. Or, indeed, the late start provides the opportunity to move things neatly to the next stage. Half-past four, however, is a disastrous time, requiring you to fill a full six and a half hours before you can reasonably slope off to bed.

I was already fearing the worst when my over-eager man arrived at the arranged time with unnerving promptness. And by 4.35 I knew it was going nowhere. He looked ridiculous, in a suit that didn't fit and with hair that didn't suit. He was twenty-three, but tried to act like he was thirty-three – to the extent that he told me he liked Katie Melua. He made a mildly racist comment. He was unattractive . . . I could go on. And on. But then I'd risk being as boring as he was.

We managed about an hour in the local pub before all topics of conversation dried up. But the blank, bored look on my face just seemed to make him even keener to spend time with me. Time.

We went back to mine. I looked at the clock. It wasn't even six o'clock. I was thinking, God, what can we do? What can we do?

I decided to cook a meal to help fill those hours up. He started saying, 'When you come to mine, I'll cook you my special' and outlining our future of constantly dining together. And I'd only known him for two – painful – hours.

When we'd finished dinner it was still only 6.30. Normally by that time you haven't even met the person. And it's better that way. I kept thinking, what can I do? I was trapped by my own inability to just tell him to leave. It would have looked too cruel. It was far too early. I was desperate. There was nothing else I could say and nothing else I could think of for us to do. It started to affect my sanity. Crazily, I thought, 'maybe if I start snogging him, time will pass more easily'. At least it was something to do rather than staring into space and trying to conceal my excruciating embarrassment.

But it was like kissing a corpse! The. Worst. Kiss. Ever. I was even more put off him – but he was really into it! What now?

My logic train had now firmly left the rails and was plunging down the ravine of unreason. I thought, 'maybe he's got a massive cock! I'll be able to entertain myself with that.' So I put my hand down his trousers. It was like a thimble. A thimble. This poor guy had everything against him.

I was thinking, 'Oh God, I can't kiss him again. It makes me a bit sick to kiss him. I can't talk to him. I don't want to go in his trousers again.'

'I think I'm falling in love with you,' he said. It was 7.30.

I told him I had to go to bed. I'm not sure if he believed me, but he left anyway – and I had a very pleasant evening to myself watching telly. Not pleasant enough to make me come round to the idea of meeting dates any earlier than nine o'clock, though.

TRIVIA

BEASTLY HABITS: SIZE MATTERS

Although male gorillas can weigh 210 kilos, their penises are usually less than 5 cm long. The Argentine lake duck, by way of contrast, weighs about 1 kg but has a 20 cm long schlong.

The biggest penis in nature award goes to the rorqual whale: up to 10 feet long. One testicle of an average blue whale, meanwhile, can weigh up to 45 kg.

However, the weirdest size difference between mates has to be the varying proportions of Green Spoon Worms. The female is 200,000 times bigger than the male. The difference between the average human and a mung bean. When she wants to reproduce, the female Green Spoon Worm sniffs up her man and inhales him into a special chamber inside her body, where he sits waiting to fertilize passing eggs.

BUTT UGLY

*M*y parents' best friends are lovely people. A great couple. So although I'm no fan of going on blind dates and had previously resisted all of my mother's attempts to snag me a 'nice young man', I felt somehow honour bound to meet the 'impressive and handsome' fellow they once lined up for me.

The dinner they arranged for us didn't go well. It wasn't so much that the man wasn't attractive and wasn't my type (although he wasn't). My real objection was that instead of making small talk, he spent most of the first course explaining and expounding upon his obsession with big round buttocks.

My embarrassment was only compounded when I had to reply to my parents' friends' eager questions about our evening together that if I'd had my way I'd have left before the main course arrived.

'But you must have talked about something?' they asked.

I didn't have the heart to tell them.

A NIGHT THAT NEVER HAPPENED

I was staying in a hotel in Limassol, Cyprus, for my sister's wedding. Working on the reception was a Cypriot lady by the name of Eleni. She had lovely black hair and green eyes, and I just had to ask her out to dinner before I left.

Trouble was, just after I'd broken the ice and we were starting to get on very well, she had a two-day rest period away from the hotel, and I didn't see her. That left just one day to move things along.

I tramped around the town, looking everywhere for a box of chocolates. Back at the hotel, I handed them to her and casually asked if she'd like to go out for a meal.

'I'm afraid I can't eat these,' she smiled. 'They will make me fat. And I'd love to go out with you, but I finish at 11 and I'm on again at 7.'

It did seem a reasonable excuse. And I became optimistic again when she asked when I had to leave and seemed genuinely disappointed that I was going so soon. She even asked me to give her my contact details and to keep in touch.

Shortly after I got back home, I wrote. There was no reply. However, as luck would have it I had to go out to Cyprus on business two months later, so I stayed at the hotel again. She wasn't there. So that was why she never answered my letters, I thought.

My positive feelings were enhanced yet further when I found out that there was a receptionist there who claimed to be a good friend of Eleni's. She also seemed to know all about me, though we'd only just met. She told me that I had only just missed seeing the object of my affection.

'Don't give up yet,' said my new friend. 'I know she wanted to see you, and she will be very upset to have missed you. I don't have her new number – but if she rings the hotel, I will get it for you.'

Again I was unlucky. I had to leave before we made contact, but the receptionist insisted that if I wrote a letter she would pass it on to Eleni.

Weeks turned into months, and still there was no reply. That's it, I thought. But out of idle curiosity I phoned the hotel to ask what had happened.

'Andy!' said the receptionist excitedly. 'Eleni's back working with us! Would you like to speak to her when she comes in?'

'I don't want to impose on her if she isn't that keen . . .'

'Don't be silly!'

And sure enough, within ten minutes Eleni was on the line. It was a relief that she sounded pleased to hear from me. She even started demanding to know why I hadn't rung. It was all to do with the time difference and working late hours, I told her, truthfully. 'But I did ask you to tell me in the letter if I could ring after 10 p.m.,' I said.

'Why don't you write to me at my home address?' she then suggested. 'Sometimes the mail gets lost here.'

So with that she gave me her home details. She also seemed pleased when I said that it would be within two weeks. 'When you come we must go out for that dinner,' she added.

The truth was, I wasn't due out on business for another ten weeks, but I didn't wanted to let things slip again and decided to go anyway. And so I found myself in Cyprus once again. I made my way to the hotel and saw she was on duty. It was late, so I decided not to bother her and left a note instead at her flat. A friendly neighbour let me in to the foyer, as there didn't seem to be a letter box. I was relieved to note that there didn't seem to be a boyfriend in residence either.

I returned to my hotel and waited for her to make contact. And waited. And waited. After the third day I knew something was seriously wrong. I went to the hotel.

As I entered the reception, I was shocked to note that there was barely a flicker of recognition from her. I asked if she got the note I left for her.

'Yes,' she replied coldly, 'but I am too busy to go out as I am working all week and have to pick my child up at 3.30 every afternoon. Anyway,' she added spitefully, 'what made you think I was interested in you?'

At this point one of the staff came into the reception. I recognized him as Stavros from the bar. He gestured at me to her. 'Who's this?' he demanded. There then followed a conversation in Greek, the gist of which seemed to be that I was no one special! Reassured, he walked off and I was left almost speechless.

Recovering a little, I demanded to know why Eleni's friend had told me that she was so keen to see me? 'She's not my friend,' she hissed, 'just a work colleague.'

It was all too much to take in. Could both of them have been playing games with me? 'I suggest you speak to her, you have her number,' spat Eleni. I protested that I didn't and was surprised that she then mellowed somewhat.

'I don't want to come to England, and I don't want any more children,' she informed me. It seemed a strange conversation to be having in the foyer when we hadn't even been for a drink.

'You must enjoy yourself while you are here,' she then added helpfully, suggesting that I might like to join in the hotel karaoke. It seemed a poor substitute for my green-eyed dream girl, especially as all the participants seemed to be retired English pensioners.

I could stand it no more and fled the hotel, hailing the nearest taxi. 'Hotel Valarna,' I barked as I settled into the front seat. With that the driver seemed to take a detour of several miles, despite the hotel being in the next block. After five minutes I tired of this, and a shouting match ensued. 'You mean "HOTEL VALAENA",' he gesticulated.

It all seemed rather academic, as there wasn't another hotel with a similar name. In the heat of the moment I left my wallet in the taxi, having paid for the large detour. Stupidly, I'd left nearly all my holiday money in it. I was left with the princely sum of a pound a day for drinks, food and entertainment. At least I could drink water and conserve my food money until more funds arrived from England, I thought.

That moment an announcement came over the hotel tannoy. 'Would all guests please purchase bottled water from the bar, due to a severe water shortage in Limassol.'

It was going to be six long days . . .

DOWN THE TOILET

*W*hen I was a student in south London, I went for a few drinks with a guy from Singapore. He seemed pretty normal until he came back to my (admittedly disgusting) shared house just off Brixton Hill.

To start with, he thought going to a scummy flat on a scummy estate was an amazing enough experience – but when he saw the loo, he actually started screaming in delight. He spurned my company in favour of taking photographs of said porcelain item to send to his friends at home. He told me excitedly that it was easily the most disgusting thing he had ever seen – and that no one in Singapore was going to BELIEVE how dirty we English are.

By the time he'd also snapped the oven, fridge and piles of dirty plates around the sink, all thoughts of sex had completely left my head – which was just as well anyway, since he refused to touch any surfaces and wouldn't even sit on the sofa for fear of getting 'germs'.

The horror and humiliation were compounded when I had to walk him down to the Underground station to get a taxi. He was too scared to go by himself. The long, cold walk wasn't made any more enjoyable by him repeatedly telling me how grateful he was for such an insight into 'dirty UK poverty' and informing me how much I'd like the loos in his country.

Recently I did go to Singapore on my way to Australia. And, yes, I did think of my erstwhile friend when I took a dump. And yes, the toilet was very nice and clean.

TRIVIA

FUNNY OLD WORLD: PLUMBING SINGAPOREAN SOCIETY

Toilets are a matter of considerable importance in Singapore. The government says clean public toilets are the hallmark of a gracious society and regularly fines people who don't flush the loo.

It isn't surprising, therefore, to learn that Singapore is also the home of the World Toilet Organization, whose stated aim is to buff up the public bathroom, and that the country hosted the world's first toilet summit in 2001.

'In the past, there were women's liberation, leprosy, AIDS, the sexual revolution. All these are taboos that have been broken. The toilet problem is probably the last one,' says Jack Sim, the president of the WTO.

But Singapore is in dire need of a sexual revolution of another kind. 'We need more babies!' says Singapore's former Prime Minister Goh Chok Tong. According to statistics for 2002, Singaporean women give birth to 1.37 babies in a lifetime – not enough to keep the population stable.

To help increase the birth rate, the Singapore government has set up a special Working Committee on Marriage and Procreation. In recent years the committee's work has included government-sponsored matchmaking efforts through its Social Development Unit (SDU for short, also known locally as 'Single, Desperate and Ugly').

One of the biggest of the SDU's initiatives is called 'Romancing

Singapore', a long-running campaign urging the islanders to 'Make Love Your Lifestyle'. As part of this programme, the Singaporean state has sponsored matchmaking events including a love boat river race, 'the lovers' challenge' (a vertical marathon in which couples run up the stairs in 43-storey office block), speed dating – in kayaks floating on a reservoir – and, oddest of all, rock climbing for couples.

Totally unrelated, but equally interesting, is the fact that nearly all pornography is forbidden by the tiny country's authoritarian regime. Censors routinely snip nudity from commercial films, and *Playboy* magazine is banned – as was the hit American TV series *Sex and the City*.

TICKED OFF

I was alone and lonely on a work assessment in a big US city, so I applied to a dating agency for similarly situated professionals. The first (and last!) date I arranged was in a restaurant. When the waiter came over and took our drinks order and I asked for wine, my date took out a sheet of paper and made a tick with an ostentatiously expensive-looking ballpoint pen.

When I asked what he was doing, he explained that he was a very busy man and that before he 'invested' too much time and 'emotional capital' in getting to know someone, he had to be sure they came up to his basic requirements.

He went on to explain his rather complicated scoring system, where you could score black marks, but where other positives, such as high income and breeding potential, could cancel them out. So I asked if ordering wine was a good or bad point. 'Bad,' he said simply.

I couldn't work out whether I felt more like a piece of meat or an interview candidate, but when he markedly folded the list and put it back in his pocket after I'd said I didn't know quite where I stood on the existence of the Trinity, I decided not to give him the satisfaction of turning me down. I wanted to storm out before he could say another word – leaving him to pay for the wine I'd just thrown in his face. Of course, I couldn't quite pluck up courage – or outrage – enough, and just sat there and took it like a fool. As well as feeling steadily more uncomfortable, I began to get a vague sense of unease. Was I so inadequate that I was even going to fail to live up to this obnoxious man's standards? The answer was of course, yes, and he never got in touch with me again. Not that I'd have replied if he had.

HACKED OFF

I spent my gap year working in a bar in the Caribbean and, while there, contracted a relationship with a diminutive but pretty blonde.

Her parents were stinking rich and had a huge house on the hill a few minutes hitch-hike from my bar. The bar was brilliant and run by a lovely family, but they did require us to sleep in a concrete cell block behind the sheds, which was overrun with cockroaches, as hot as an oven and infested with the pubes of a thousand previous itinerant gap-year bums. I was therefore even keener than I might otherwise have been to get on good terms with my sweetheart's parents, so I could spend my nights ensconced with their daughter in the splendid, cool confines of her luxury pad.

One night the lovely girl invited me to dinner at her house. It was a proper 'meet the parents' occasion and thoroughly nerve-wracking.

Perhaps I should explain at this point that I wasn't just going to have to butter up the parents; I also had a lot of ground to claw back. Earlier on in my relationship with their daughter I had been caught in the house *in flagrante delicto* by my inamorata's younger sister. This had occasioned much laughter and embarrassment at the time, but her mum remained very disturbed by it. Her father was a genial giant who loved nothing better than catching big fat sharks, and while he liked me socially, this recent incident had also

49

reminded him rather pointedly that I was in fact knobbing his little girl.

Anyway, I prepared for the evening with care and attention to show I really did hold their daughter in esteem. I wore a fresh, clean shirt, and even washed and ran a comb through my matted locks. I turned up on the porch at the appointed hour and ooh'd and aah'd over the house as if I had never been in there and had never been caught pounding their eldest doggy-style on the leopard-skin rug.

Her mum behaved erratically and stared accusingly at first, but she began to soften as the young lady and I talked amiably about our plans to carry on the relationship after I went up to university and so forth. I brown-nosed her dad about fishing and even secured an invitation on the next trip. I was really making headway, and my girl gave me an appreciative ball-squeeze as I carried the dishes through to the kitchen.

Next up, the veranda. A staple of Caribbean living if you are a millionaire and your daughter is sleeping with a plausible but definitely amoral young whelp is to retire after dinner to the veranda, roll a gigantic joint and give him a gentle grilling.

Since big spliffs and small talk were two of my fortes, I was now well and truly relaxing into the final furlong. I had even planned to go home fairly early in the evening in order to underline my respect for the house. But I was happily picturing nights spent under the high ceilings and ever-rotating brass fans of this impressive *pied-à-terre*.

The chat was going amiably enough, and her mum was, understandably, digging a bit into my past, future and intentions towards her daughter. I could cope with all this easily enough because I was solidly middle-class, heading for Oxford and a born liar.

Next up – careers.

'What would you like to do after Oxford?' asked my prospective mother-in-law.

'Oh, I dunno. I suppose I could follow the family footsteps and be a journalist.'

'You mean, like those hell hounds that drove Diana into an early grave?' came the rejoinder.

Now, she was an intelligent woman, everyone was stoned, I knew that the Princess of Hearts was a gak-snuffing *über*-bimbo now dead for over six months, and I thought this was probably a joke. Even if it wasn't, she'd just heard me say my family were hacks, so I thought a mild joke back would do the trick.

'Oh, something like that. Maybe not a paparazzi, but definitely in the gutter tabloid line.'

She tried to kill me there and then on her veranda. She eventually had to be restrained by her husband. The woman was shrieking at me like a banshee and actually succeeded in clawing my cheek, hitting me with an ashtray and knocking her husband down before I fled, never to be invited back.

TRIVIA

DOOMED LOVE: OSCAR AND BOSIE

Few parents have been as successful at ruining their offspring's love lives as the Marquess of Queensberry, the man who put the kibosh on the famous love affair between his son Lord Alfred Douglas (known to his friends as Bosie) and Oscar Wilde.

Queensberry first tried to scupper the men's relationship by stalking them everywhere they went. When this failed, he threatened to disrupt the premiere of Wilde's play *The Importance of Being*

Earnest. But Wilde hired guards to keep the angry old man outside the theatre, leaving him humiliated, pacing outside the theatre with a bouquet of vegetables and no one to receive them.

Rounds 1 and 2 to Oscar. But the aristocratic pugilist – a renowned prize-fighter who also, famously, devised the Queensberry boxing rules – had always been one to battle furiously until the last bell. He finally got the poor poet on the ropes when he provoked Oscar into suing him for libel by leaving his calling card, complete with the legend 'To Oscar Wilde, posing as a somdomite' (*sic*).

Wilde lost the case and was himself charged with homosexual offences. He got two years' hard labour in Reading Gaol. He was bankrupted and ostracized by London society and died not long after his release in 1900.

As ever, however, Victorian society's greatest self-declared genius had the last laugh. 'I shall never makes a new friend in life, though I rather hope to make a few in death,' he'd declared after his fall from grace, a prophecy that has come true a million times over, history regarding Wilde as one of the paragons of his age and the Marquess of Queensberry as a ridiculous, not to mention nasty, old homophobe.

DO YOU KNOW WHO I AM?

I was happy to have pulled someone who, if not quite an A-list celeb, was at the time still very prominent on the UK airwaves. I'd been slightly put off when, after we'd had sex, he suggested that we 'basked in the afterglow', but I still kind of thought he was OK.

So I was quite pleased when he wanted to follow up and took me for a drink in the Park Lane Hilton. We went up to the top floor, where he said there was a bar from which you could see half of London. A nice polite lady let us in, and we sat down by the window. The view was indeed unbelievable. I didn't have long to enjoy it, however, because the bar manager came over and said, 'I'm very sorry, but you're going to have to leave.'

It turned out that our footwear – trainers – wasn't suitable for such an elevated drinks establishment. I wasn't bothered, but my semi-famous friend looked outraged. The woman who'd let us in was desperately trying to apologize, but my date wasn't having any of it, preferring instead to work himself up into more and more of a frenzy with her and the bar manager. The next thing I knew, he was screaming, 'DO YOU KNOW WHO I AM???' They weren't sure. So we had to leave.

To calm him down, I took him for a walk across Hyde Park. But then someone accidentally bumped into him and he was off again. 'GOD DAMN IT, YOU FAT BASTARD!' he started yelling as the poor tourist tried to waddle away. 'DON'T YOU . . .'

I decided we'd better get a taxi home. Unfortunately, the driver of the first cab we flagged down refused to go to Kentish Town. Apparently, drivers aren't allowed to refuse a fare if their taxi lights are on, and my broadcaster companion was soon off again, reading the 'Cockney Cunt' the riot act.

'DO YOU EVEN FUCKING KNOW WHO I AM?' he asked again.

'No. Fuck off,' said the cabbie and drove off into the night.

I decided to catch a Tube home. Alone.

A MUG'S GAME

*C*lare and I were both pretty excited and nervous to be going to a well-known Manchester club. We were young enough for the experience of going to a big, famous night-club to be still pretty daunting, and it was our first date. Although our lips had briefly brushed when she'd agreed to come with me, we'd really barely even touched each other. I was hoping that a night of debauchery and dancing in Manchester's finest would change all that and I'd finally get to know the girl intimately.

We had a great meal beforehand, and when our hands met in the back of the taxi on the way to the club I almost shouted in happiness. Things were going damn well . . . until, that is, a car bumped into the back of us, just after we'd turned into the dark lanes of the industrial estate where the club was situated. Our driver screeched to a halt with a curse, only realizing his mistake when a man in a balaclava ran up and tapped on the window. With a gun.

Soon this man was established in the front seat. Another man wearing a sock over his head and also holding what looked like a gun was sitting next to us. We were driving away from our intended nightspot while this second fellow chatted away amiably, doing a pretty passable Liam Gallagher impression.

'Now then. Safe. Yeah. Sorry to spoil your night, like, but it's business, innit? Sound. We're going on a little tour around the sights and sounds of this great city now. First we'll go to a couple of cash points and you'll give us all your money. Are you all right in the front there? Fucking hell! Calm the fuck down!'

Our taxi driver, who was now sweating profusely, had just run a red light.

'You've got a long way to drive yet, mate. It's going to be a while before we have to smash your car up. Isn't that right, Our Kid?'

His friend prodded the driver with the gun so he got the message.

Now my date was crying silently. I suppose in a sense I'd got what I wanted as she was clinging to my arm, but I have to say things weren't ideal.

Pretty soon we were both £250 worse off, having been marched up to a cash point and made to empty out our accounts. We then tore around some of the dodgiest parts of Manchester, stopping off outside various flats and shady-looking pubs so that the guy from the front seat could disappear inside to do I-shudder-to-think-what, while his friend stayed in the back with us, his gun trained on our poor driver.

It could have been worse, though. Our kidnappers were at least nice, polite and chatty all evening (demands for money and holding us against our will aside). They told us plenty of jokes, discussed the football at length, and one of them even brought us some chocolate when he used some of our money to buy petrol for the taxi.

Still, by 4 a.m. my date and I were both exhausted and numb with fear, and our abductors' behaviour was getting increasingly erratic. It was probably the greatest relief of my life when they finally let us go.

To add insult to injury, just before they sped away in the stolen car, one of our bad lads wound down the window, pointed his gun in the air and pulled the trigger. A small blue flame came out. It was a novelty cigarette lighter.

Clare didn't laugh when I suggested that we do the same again next week. But not all was lost, as I'm happy to say we've been married for three years now.

TRIVIA

LOVE HURTS: SEX SIGNALS

An article published in *New Scientist* magazine suggests that the best way to meet a lover is to experience fear with them. An experiment in the 1970s found that men who met women on a rickety bridge found the encounter sexier than those that met on a stable bridge. Funfair rides have a similar effect – prospective partners look more attractive to people who have just got off a roller-coaster.

The other five top ways to create attraction are said to come through body language (mirroring a partner's gestures is said to be particularly effective, crossing arms especially off-putting), sharing a joke and laughter, eating chocolate (which releases the 'love molecule' the chemical phenylethylamine in the brain), lingering eye contact and, inexplicably, listening to soft rock together. Apparently psychologists at North Adams state college in Massachusetts discovered that women found pictures of men more attractive when they were listening to power ballads.

CHEAP AND CHEERLESS

I had been going out with this guy for about six weeks when I realized that our personalities were too different for our relationship to work. But when I tried to tell him that we had to split up, he looked mortified. Torn apart he was. He begged and pleaded for one more chance to make a go of things. Being the nice girl that I am, I agreed.

When the big night came, he arrived with a gift. My initial delight was dulled slightly when I noticed that it was wrapped in Christmas paper (this was the beginning of February, after all), but I tore at the packaging happily enough, wondering what it could contain. Of course, I could never have imagined what it actually turned out to be – a remote-controlled plastic car.

He then proceeded to tell me how much it had cost him, saying the label had said it was reduced from £20 to £10, but he still wasn't going to get it until the man at the till in the shop had told him he could have it for £3.

You can imagine how special that made me feel, but I still didn't properly get the message until he said he'd also lined up a 'romantic meal' for two for our Sunday lunch – and drove me to the local supermarket café.

SINS OF THE FATHER

I'd gone with some friends to the bar in one of the university colleges in Oxford. I separated from them, however, when a darkly handsome man started stroking my leg at the bar. Full to the brim with alcohol, and feeling more than a little horny myself, I readily accepted his suggestion that we go for a 'walk'.

I'd assumed that he was a member of the college and we'd just go back to his room, but it turned out he wasn't, and his plan was to do it in the bushes and just hope they didn't have CCTV.

I thought this was a splendid idea – the naughtiness and excitement adding just the right frisson to my mood. We wandered around the grounds for a while, near a gate that led to the garden, waiting for someone to unlock it so we could quickly follow him or her in.

Soon we were inside, under a suitable bush and very much *in flagrante delicto*. The brief oral sex actually turned out to be rather disappointing, however, and afterwards we both felt more than a little awkward with each other. A mood that was by no means enhanced when we realized that the gate leading out of the garden was firmly shut and there was no one around to help us get through it.

I had my mobile phone and wanted to ring the college porter, but my companion said no. He was too afraid of getting into trouble for being in the garden when we shouldn't have been.

So we stood there for over almost an hour. Shivering. Not talking. It was really awkward. There wasn't even anywhere to sit. And my pants were feeling rather soiled. Eventually, the silence just became unbearable.

'So what do you do?' I asked in a desperate attempt at small talk.

'I'd rather not say,' he replied, looking away from me.

'Oh come on. Don't be shy,' I cajoled him. 'My job's not glamorous. I'm an accountant, for God's sake.'

'Well, if you must know, I'm a trainee priest.'

Ten minutes later – ten very long minutes later – someone came to the gate and we were able to escape. We didn't even say goodbye to each other.

TRIVIA

BEYOND BELIEF: THE PROSTITUTES' PADRE

The Revd Harold Davidson, rector of the aptly named Stiffkey, became famous in the 1930s for his work with fallen women – especially young and attractive ones, whom, rumour had it, he often actually helped to fall.

Known as 'the prostitutes' padre', he was banned from tea-shops across London because of his repeated attempts to snag waitresses by showing them a picture of an actress who he said had come to him to be 'saved'. However, he met with more success when he approached a sixteen-year-old prostitute called Barbara Harris with the winning question 'Has anyone ever told you that you look like the film actress Mary Brian?'

Davidson's downfall came when another of his fallen women, Rose Ellis (a prostitute he'd had close contact with for more than ten years while trying to save her soul), was convinced by a detective and several glasses of port to reveal the secrets of their relationship. Davidson appeared in court charged with adultery. The case went against him when the prosecution produced a picture of the naughty vicar with a naked girl, a fifteen-year-old whom Davidson had taken under his wing on the understanding that he would help her career as a swimsuit model.

He was defrocked shortly afterwards and started a new career exhibiting himself in a barrel on Blackpool promenade. His attempts to clear his name were finally cut short when he was fatally mauled by a lion called Freddy, in Skegness.

A HEAVY BLOW

*W*hen I was a drunken teenage Heavy Metal fan, I often found myself seeing dodgy groups in grotty venues where the only way to make yourself heard to girls you were trying to chat up was to yell really loudly above the noise of the band. But when you're drunk and a teenager, disaster always lurks around the corner, particularly if your conversational bons mots have no chance of being heard above the background roar.

So it was that during a gig by Thrash Metal pioneers Nuclear Assault, Glasgow Rooftops *circa* 1988, I was having trouble making myself noticeable to a girl. Suddenly a drunken hard noise fan threw up while trying to get by. Immediately a large circle of people trying to avoid the vomit opened up between me and my target female.

I took myself off to the bar to curse my ill luck. Amazingly enough, though, the girl in question followed me, and in my teenage excitement I said to her something along the lines of 'Are you trying to avoid the sick?' Immediately I was on the receiving end of one of the most tremendous punches I've ever received. Worse still, in those days I was incredibly prone to nose bleeds. The blood gushed out, and I yelled, 'What the hell did you do that for?' and the girl said, 'There's no way I'll suck your dick.'

THE DEVIL'S WORK

*A*s a student, I was involved in the theatre group at university – purely as a way to meet girls. So when I managed to persuade one to go out with me on a date, the natural thing to do was to go to the theatre. It would show how artistic, sensitive and know-ledgeable I was, while also providing us with a natural conversa-tional topic in the pub afterwards – and what with both of us being amateur actors, what could possibly go wrong?

Well what went wrong was that the play I took my first date to was a stage version of Dennis Potter's *Brimstone and Treacle*. I had no idea at the time what happens in that play. The date went fine right up to the point where the son of Satan rapes the disabled woman on stage – conveniently enough, just before the interval. The conversation was somewhat stilted and date no. 2 didn't happen. Next time I managed to get a girl to go out with me, I believe a film starring Julia Roberts may have been involved . . .

NEED FOR SPEED?

I met a man – let's call him Charlie – at speed dating. He seemed kind of twitchy, which I thought was nerves, but when we went out on our first date, he continued to be quite manic. I also noticed that he made many, many visits to the toilet.

On date 2 Charlie went to the loo for the second time in under an hour and I texted a friend while I waited. I wanted to let him know that I had just seen a mutual friend, but I added in: 'My date is in the toilet. He does that a lot. I think he might be a junkie.'

Needless to say, I was horrified when I then realized I had accidentally sent the text to Charlie instead of my chum. Charlie emerged from the toilet, sniffing very exaggeratedly and toying with his nose. Naturally, I pretended I had sent him the text as a joke.

I can't help feeling Charlie may have had the last laugh, however, as on date 3, immediately after sex at his place, he switched on the TV and started watching football. When I said 'Do we have to have this on?' he asked 'Why? Is there something you want to watch on the other side?'

NO OIL IN THE TANK

*G*iorgio had asked me on a dinner date. The idea was that I'd get a taxi to his house and then he'd drive us on to a restaurant. I got in the taxi all right, but part 2 of the plan was quickly jettisoned. We had a pre-dinner drink on the sofa and got talking. Soon we were kissing lustily. We got so carried away that we didn't even check the time until it was past midnight – and we'd completely missed all chance of getting a meal.

Since there was nothing else for it – and because we were both very much in the mood, it seemed like the natural choice to take things to the next stage.

Things got steamy, and I was beginning to think that it was going to be a great night until Giorgio's manhood failed – midway through. Missing dinner had been a terrible mistake, he said, as he had hardly eaten all day, and now his blood sugar was too low for him to perform to his usual high standard.

Practical and undeterred, I marched him to the kitchen for a snack. No such luck. The man had NOTHING to eat in his house. Not a biscuit, not a crumb, not even a beer.

OK, now what? We shrugged our shoulders and tried to put some pulse back into his pants . . . things got steamy . . . and then, flop, it happened again.

This time I was undeterred, as was he. After a few minutes' break we started up again. The third and fourth time I was still easily cajoled into thinking this was just a momentary wobble – and that we could do something about it. But after that things started to look a bit more desperate. It became embarrassing. I started wanting to give up for the night, just cuddle or do something else, give it a few days' time. But oh no. Giorgio was, after all, Italian and, as he explained to me, Italian men are not to be easily separated from their virility. Macho Giorgio was NOT letting me go home until I'd been 'satisfied'. He was decidedly NOT about to drive me back. He did NOT even want to let me out of the bed, until he had PROVEN himself to me.

I was being held hostage by his sexual ego, and there was no escape. By 4 a.m. I had tried everything I could think of to arouse him, lull him to sleep, convince him, plead with him, threaten him, anything so I could just go home. Finally, out of what must have been pure boredom, he acquiesced, pulled on his trousers and walked to the car . . . which had no oil. It was as if the universe was trying to supply a metaphor.

Giorgio didn't find the irony all that amusing. What's more, he said, since we couldn't drive (either), I was just going to have to spend the night. Not on your life, I thought, and I rummaged around his garage in the dark until I found some oil. Just enough for the car to rattle and shuffle its way slowly across town to my house, where at 6 a.m., I fell into bed exhausted, if not exactly satiated. As I drifted into blissful sleep, I vowed never EVER to go near a macho Italian man again – until the next time, anyway.

TRIVIA

BEASTLY HABITS: BAD SEX

It takes rats, ducks and kangaroos 3 minutes to copulate. Whales and elephants take 30 seconds. Male chimpanzees can reach climax in about 10 seconds. Mice can do it in 5. Mosquitoes in 2–3 seconds. Male stick insects, in contrast, will mate with their partner for up to 10 weeks, refusing to dismount no matter how hard she tries to shake him off.

The male honeybee doesn't have such a good experience. For a start, there can be up to 25,000 other bees competing for the same Queen Bee – which will probably mate fewer than 20 times in its lifetime. Not surprisingly, most male honeybees die virgins. And if they do succeed in snagging the Queen, they die right away. That's because, when the male honeybee ejaculates, his genitals are torn from his body with an audible snap – and he explodes.

At least the poor bee has a better fate than the male praying mantis. Females generally tear off their spouse's head before they have sex, leaving the brainless torso thrashing around at her rear end – which probably goes to prove something . . . although quite what is a whole different question.

But even the praying mantis can consider himself lucky compared to the unfortunate male midge. Once the female of the species has caught him, she plunges her proboscis into his head and her spittle turns his innards to soup, which she then sucks out, before casting away the dried out husk of a man when she's done – but not before the male midge's manhood has broken off inside her.

And if you think all of that's bad, spare a thought for *Philodina roseola*, aka the bdelloid rotifer. No members of this species have had any sex at all for over 85 million years, since the last males of the species disappeared. The female-only species reproduces by cloning.

DR LOVE

I've always had a bit of a thing for doctors, so when I got on well with the dishy-looking 'Dr J.' at a rather amateurish – but fun – speed dating evening arranged by some girlfriends of mine, he was the first one I ticked. He'd ticked me too, so we arranged to meet the following week in a restaurant. Before we'd even got through the starter, my evening with George Clooney turned into a bad sitcom when a lady at the table opposite us started to choke.

I thought it was my big chance to see my medical man in action. I'd always had a kind of daydream fantasy about being the thrilled spectator as my lover's healing hands saved someone's life . . . except that he didn't seem to be doing much about this poor sputtering woman at all.

'Aren't you going to help her?' I demanded.

'What?'

'That woman over there – she's practically turning blue.'

'God. Oh dear. Christ. Yes, I'll get a waiter to call for an ambulance.'

'Why don't you just help her?'

He looked baffled and frightened, especially when I started tugging on his sleeve. Luckily, just as I was about to start trying to force my date out of his chair, the woman gave a huge hacking bellow and started to recover of her own accord. I say 'luckily' because, as my date explained when he'd finally worked out what I'd been going on about, he was a university lecturer with a doctorate in medieval history, and the only time he'd been in a hospital was to have his appendix removed.

IN THE DOG HOUSE

I like dogs plenty. I've got a Labrador now, and it doesn't even sadden me to say that, aside from my wife, he's probably my best friend in the world. I can't stand Jack Russell terriers though. Rat-sized, constantly yelping, scuttling, demonically evil critters. Walking advertisements for steel-toed boots. I hate them.

OK, I admit it. I'm biased. But then, one of them did once shit on my head.

It was the first time I'd gone back to my (then) new girlfriend's house, and things had been going well. Our cosy session on the sofa had been occasionally interrupted by her pair of yapping little smelly dog blighters, but nothing too bad. I'd even laughed along when one of them had started playing tug-of-war with my sock and – since said sock was still on my foot – nipping my toes in the process. Nor had the all-important 'mood' been irreparably damaged when the object of my affection had switched hers to the dogs, cooing at them for ten minutes and apologizing profusely to them because they couldn't come and sleep with 'Mummy' in her bedroom quite yet . . .

Upstairs, behind closed doors, things had gone even better. I was soon enjoying the blissful sleep of the tired and happy. I was briefly woken once by the sounds of the door opening, scuttling feet, more cooing and the sensation of something licking my ear, but I soon drifted off again. A happy chappy.

Then I got that funny feeling. The one you get when you're still asleep but start to become aware of something going on in the real world outside your dreams. This something was accompanied by wheezing, snorting and vague straining sounds. Then I felt a sensation like a warm and damp tongue brushing against my forehead with feathery lightness.

I must have instinctively brushed my hand up to see what it was, because the feeling of clammy goo against my fingers hit me at the same time as the overpowering smell. I'd been shat on.

The ensuing scene of dry retching, frantic rushing for the bathroom, swearing about that fucking little rat-dog and my partner's cries of 'naughty Mimsy' need hardly be described. Suffice to say that it was weeks before I felt fully clean again. And no, I didn't go back there.

AN UNORDERED MAIN COURSE

*H*e was a friend of a friend, someone I had been introduced to once briefly at a party. This friend (the one we were both friends of – not him – if you catch my drift) had ordered him to take care of me after my move to a new city, and so he invited me to dinner at his house. He had put in quite a bit of effort, and the three courses all looked delicious.

I was expecting a nice chat, a meal, some tips on restaurants, cinemas and bus routes and then to go home for an early night. I hadn't quite realized how different his intentions were until, shortly after taking the starter dishes back to the kitchen, he leaped on me, pushed me to the wall and started frantically kissing me. I was stunned.

It was all wrong, too. I am tall, and he was short: at his full height he just about reached my shoulder. He was frantic, manic, obviously in the throes of some passionate eruption that I hadn't seen coming. The effect was quite like being mauled by a gerbil.

I didn't know what to do, so I didn't do anything. I just let him belabour me with his tongue, until he finally decided to whisper huskily into my ear that we should maybe take this upstairs. Appalled at the thought but still in shock, I only managed a weak 'Oh, no, shouldn't we finish dinner?'

Luckily, at that moment his housemate arrived, causing him to jump up guiltily and pretend nothing had happened. We finished our food in a far more civilized manner. I got my tips on restaurants, cinemas and bus routes, and I went home for a nice early night.

GETTING CRABBY

*T*here was a rumour going round my Cambridge college about a crabs infestation. I was very worried, not least because my flat-mate was supposed to be its source and I'd lazily used his towel that very morning when I'd been unable to locate mine.

Now he was away in London, without his mobile phone, and I was already beginning to feel itchy. Was it just psychological? Was I the new home for millions of pubic lice? God, it was getting me down. And I was supposed to be going to a party in about an hour. And I had been hoping to pull a girl I'd fancied for months. And now I couldn't. Nor could I very well explain that the reason I was suddenly about to go cold on her was that I had a venereal disease.

I needed cheering up. So when my mate suggested we do a pill, I took two.

The Ecstasy did its work, and by the time we arrived at the party I was feeling good – very good indeed. All that itching was just a distant memory. I was horny again. And full of love for everyone in the room. Especially the girl I liked. So when she suggested that we go for a walk along the Backs in the moonlight, I felt like the happiest man alive.

The walk was quite wonderful. The only thing more beautiful than the silent colleges and the moon on the water of the still river was the wondrous creature beside me. I just wanted to hug and kiss her all night long. I felt all warm and emotional inside, and I was so overcome with excitement and gratitude when she asked me back to her room that I almost wept.

The trouble was, I realized as a wave of drug-induced paranoia washed over me just before we started having sex, that I'd forgotten that I was carrying a VD. I felt horror and remorse. This lovely, beautiful, perfect girl had trusted me, and I had been about to betray her. I was a bad, bad man. I had to be honest with her. I had to.

And that's why I whispered lovingly into her ear, 'I'm really sorry, but I've got crabs.'

Of course, it turned out that the rumour was nothing more than that – a rumour. I'd never had any kind of VD at all. But by the time I worked all that out, however, I'd already made an ignominious early exit from my amorous endeavours and been told in the clearest possible terms never to trouble the (no longer) prospective love of my life again.

STAR-CROSSED LOVER

I think every young man has fantasies about high-cheeked Slavic maidens – or at least I did. So when I realized that my job was boring, that girls were not as permissive in the UK as I might like, and that I could get 50 roubles to the pound, I decided to go to Russia.

Things didn't go too well, however, since I was a bit of a drunk who neither knew the Russian alphabet (not at first, anyway) nor cared particularly about the noble Russian soul, and consequently I found talking to girls pretty difficult.

I lived with two Americans, one of whom was a good-natured if slightly goofy jock, the other an obsessive-compulsive chain-smoker who wanted to be British so much that he had adopted the habit of speaking Dickensian English and singing 'God Save the Queen' every time he drank. Verily, it was a shag pad.

My flatmates and I all taught at schools around St Petersburg. I taught children. Wrong to hit on. They taught adults. Right to hit on. Or at least, less wrong.

Over potatoes and water one dinnertime 'Obsessive-compulsive' dropped in the fact that he had organized a party with three beautiful Russian girls he'd met at work. I immediately had images of Bacchanalian orgies with me wearing a toga, being fed grapes and with conversation at a minimum (me occasionally saying 'I am mighty Zeus; get me more wine'). However, I think he envisaged a

Russian literature book club with a sprinkling of chat about the wonderful paintings in the Hermitage.

Well, the big day arrived. I had got slightly too 'refreshed' the night before to be able to contemplate cooking and cleaning, so I had to leave it to the other two. That was a mistake. I woke up expecting the house spick and span. Not only was it still as black as night in there, but also there was no food whatsoever.

Imagining that my flatmates had it all in hand, I grabbed a pile of cash from the kitchen table and went to buy some Georgian wine and cheap champagne. It was only when I got back that I realized that the money I'd taken was for our supper – the Americans had been planning to go to the Russian equivalent of Domino's for pizza. I realized this fact, because they were, as they put it, thoroughly 'pissed' with me. I didn't mind too much until I realized that with the change we could only afford two pizzas between six of us.

I was worried. Not propitious circumstances for love. Bad vibes and an empty stomach. I felt even more concerned when the first two 'lovelies' shimmied through the door. It was like the collective farms' most experienced, prize potato pickers had just taken a wrong turn and wandered into my life. What's more, they wanted to be fed, watered and amused. There was a lurking suspicion in my mind that they might 'hulk out' if this was not forthcoming.

I was feeling morose. But then the third girl came in. Sveta. Young, attractive, Russian. Jackpot!

After some stilted initial conversation I found that Girls 1 and 2 were English teachers, so they not only understood everything I said, but they also had textbook expectations of the 'English gentleman'. Curses.

Not being a team player, I let the Americans handle those two and moved on to the luminous Sveta. Not only was she hot, but she also rented a room to one of the other girls. She was rich!

Our understanding of each other was limited by a language barrier, but I managed to let her know that I liked drinking and was not very good at Russian. She managed to inform me that she was spiritual (star signs and stuff) and not very good at English.

We let the others talk art and culture while we let the international language of booze and cheap tobacco flow like sweet, sweet wine. When we graduated on to shot-drinking competitions and trying to get alcohol poisoning, the others polished off the pizza and decided to go for a walk around the city.

When they told me they were leaving, I felt elated. Aphrodite was giving me a break for once, and the lack of comprehension meant no tortured post-coital analysis and a quick get-away. Hooray. I was happy.

Sveta and I finished the wine and, with nothing better to do, we started getting 'comfortable'. That's a euphemism. She was still babbling about star signs, the sky at night, hippy shit, but I didn't care – I wasn't getting images of Patrick Moore.

I had already made it clear to this girl that I wasn't an 'English gentleman'. I was instead a Scottish barbarian. I proudly tried to fulfil this stereotype and attempted to shepherd her into my palatial bedroom. She playfully shook her head before suggesting with words and motions that we go for a romantic river walk.

No alarm bells yet. It's romantic, I was thinking. There's nice scenery, and the fresh air will clear my head and enhance my performance – as well as my chance of getting second helpings. (For those who are finding my thought patterns disgracefully sexist, by the way, I could defend myself by saying that I hadn't had any lady-time for about six months . . . although, on reflection, I guess that it might be this very attitude that explains why.)

Anyway, we stumbled out into the Russian night. It was cold, but not that bad. Indeed, it was hand-holding and getting-cosy weather. We started walking down the river, and she suggested that we went to her flat near Hermitage Square. Cool, I thought.

So we continued to walk hand in hand, gazing at the stars and murmuring sweet incomprehensible nothings into each other's ears. Orion truly shone brightly that night.

I thought romance still lingered in the air as we made it to her flat complete with bottles of lager and cigarettes, which she had paid for. (Sex, free alcohol and not even having to host. Wow, I was like a pig in shit.)

Cigarettes were lit, and we opened a couple of beers. She beckoned me into her room – everything was going delightfully quickly. But then she sat down at her computer. Strange. My addled brain was hoping that she had some outlandish Russian hardcore to show me, so I was disappointed when this astrological map came up. Then the questions began.

She said she needed to know my full name and how to spell it, my date of birth, time of birth, birth stone, favourite colour, first pet. It was all I could do with my poor Russian to even answer one thing. It was like the KGB conducting an interview with a half-wit to make him confess to torching the Politburo's new scout hut. Plus, not being a great believer in that sort of astrological stuff, I had to make it all up.

As the information was processed, I realized what she was doing – she had profiled herself exactly, and every time I answered a question her profile altered in perspective. She was trying to find out if the Delta of Venus was in my quadrant tonight, and I was trying to facilitate this with a lethal lottery of untruths. FUCK!!!! My lies had better be the right answers, was all I was hoping.

The questioning finished, she pressed a processing button and then led me to the kitchen, where she sat me down, told me to wait and got me another beer.

Five minutes passed, and she came through with a flicker of a smile on her face. We talked for a few minutes, shared a cigarette and kissed. I passed! I'm the cleverest man in the universe! I am god of sex! Garnet is my birth stone! I was coming up on lies . . . and loving it. That was, until she said, 'Now you must go.'

I was so shocked I didn't even try the subtle arts of persuasion to reverse the decision. My jaw hit the floor and she escorted me to the door, crushed.

I wandered out onto the street, where it was now −5° C. I was wearing just a jumper, the place was crawling with police and not a cab to be found. The humiliation still lives with me.

CHEESY KNOB

This is going back a few years, but I was once having a Friday night drink at a bar called Frevd, in Oxford. I was with a gang of people, one of whom was a chap called Laurence. I'd never met Laurence before, but he and I were getting on splendidly. The talk was flowing as fast as the wine: lots of mutual connections, same sense of humour, similar interests etc., etc. Then, during a brief lull in the conversation, I began to say, 'I really fancy a cheesy dance.' However, I'd obviously had one too many by then, and what actually came out was 'I really fancy a cheesy knob.'

Laurence laughed along with me, but the moment was broken. I disappeared on to the dance floor and was never to see him again, let alone discover whether his todger was cheesy or not.

BIBLE BASHED

*W*hen she'd asked me out, Sheila had suggested that we first go to a gathering of a few friends of hers, who were, she said, 'really nice, really lovely, good people'. I said yes at once. I fancied Sheila something chronic – as did everyone else on my floor at work (who made no attempt to hide their jealousy that I'd snagged 'the fit one from accounts'). Sheila may have dressed conservatively, but there was no hiding that gorgeous body. And while her face might not have launched a thousand ships, it certainly floated my boat.

So I'd happily ignored the warning bells ringing in my sub-conscious about the presence of all those other 'lovely people'. I even reasoned that they could help diffuse a potentially awkward situation in the event of any personality clash between me and my date. Everything was going to be just fine. Or so I thought.

Of course, looking back, I should have realized that there was something unusual about being invited to a café next to a religious bookshop rather than a pub. And with the benefit of hindsight I can see that the one conversation I'd managed to have with Sheila that had got beyond small talk about the weather wasn't exactly indicative of a future of unlimited fun and rumpy-pumpy. She'd asked me whether I thought I was a good and happy person and something about God. If I'm honest, I can't quite remember the details as I was so busy gawping at her décolletage, the contents of which were so striking I was blinded to all other warning signs.

I didn't even catch on when I arrived at the café (or at least, I did my best to keep my brain in its state of blissful ignorance) and saw that all the seats had been arranged in a circle – and were already all occupied by her 'friends'. These people were nearly all wearing patterned jumpers and had faces distinguished only by their lifeless white puffiness and earnest expressions. Sarah looked like a sunbeam by comparison – and I basked in her light when she introduced me as 'someone new, someone who I know is very special'. I felt another little warm glow when she added, flashing me her brilliant blonde-girl smile, 'And he's looking for love.'

But, of course, this warm feeling soon turned to an icy chill. I was finally forced to admit to myself that I was at a Bible meeting rather than a date when everyone in the circle started holding hands and a man with two days' stubble, ear-rings and a torn denim jacket suggested that, before we started, we should say a quick prayer.

Sheila flashed me her adorable smile again and squeezed my hand, and everyone else looked at me so earnestly that I was really tempted to stay. But when the prayer was over and the trendy vicar looked long and lingeringly into my eyes and asked me if I knew about heaven and knew if I was going there, I stammered out my excuses and headed for the door. My exit was made all the swifter by the fact I'd now spotted the guitar and tambourine in the corner.

Sheila was now keeping completely silent. She only nodded furiously as Mr Ear-rings warned me that the door out of the café was the door into hell. He'd got that right, at least, I reflected as I hot-footed it down the street. I did live in Bradford at the time, after all.

My feelings of humiliation and embarrassment were only compounded when everyone else on my floor at work revealed that they hadn't really been jealous of me at all, being fully aware that the only man Sheila would ever allow into her life was Jesus. They were all highly amused that I'd let her take me to 'meet him'.

TRIVIA

BEYOND BELIEF: FLIRTY FISHING

In the 1970s the Children of God cult developed a recruitment technique called 'flirty fishing'. Attractive female members of the group were told to 'lure in a fish', using themselves as bait. Men were told to give up their wives as a symbol of their devotion to the cause. These 'Happy Hookers for Jesus' were even sent knocking on doors like Jehovah's Witnesses – but they offered something more than a look at *The Watchtower*.

GOING BANANAS

*M*y mate Pete had arranged to meet up with a woman he'd fancied for a while, but he'd heard nothing from her for a few days. Ignoring friends' advice to forget about it, he decided to go to the pub where they had planned to meet, just in case.

While in this slightly dodgy pub, with a book for company, he was interrupted by a drunk woman – obviously semi-resident there – who slapped a banana down on the bar next to him with the words, 'What do you think of that, then?'

He tried to be polite for several minutes while the unfortunate woman made continued attempts to strike up apparently fruit-related conversation. Eventually, he cracked and said, 'Would you mind fucking off? I'm just here for a quiet drink.' The barman looked at him and winced, knowing only too well what might be coming.

The woman shouted at him for some minutes, without seeming to draw breath or approach coherence even briefly, before – finally – giving up and going to sit on the opposite side of the pub, where she contented herself by simply bellowing the word 'banana' at random intervals across the room.

A little later he got an unexpected call from the woman he'd made the date with. She was sorry she hadn't been in touch, but she was going out for drinks with some friends – did he want to join them? The answer was yes, of course, but with the proviso that they meet in a different pub from the one he was in right now.

Half an hour or so later, she and some friends came into the second pub, and she greeted him with the words every man loves to hear: 'Have you met my boyfriend?'

He stayed for long enough to ensure that it didn't look like he was storming off, and no longer. As soon as it seemed OK, he went to his usual cab firm down the road to order a ride home. While there, the man behind the desk, who he always spoke to, asked him out. He let the guy down as gently as he could manage, given how much he'd had to drink, and how disappointing his night had already been in so many ways.

BORN IN A BARN

*M*y friends laughed at me for going on a Scottish country dancing evening for a first date. I was a bit apprehensive myself, but actually the girl in question and I both enjoyed it greatly. It turned out that there's nothing like bit of tomfoolery to ancient traditional instruments to get your guard down. Well, that and all the beer you have to drink before you can face dancing.

So we got a bit smashed, danced about holding hands with all sorts of people . . . and then went back to my place. It went well. A most successful evening, until my date started sleepwalking in the middle of the night, wandered over to the corner of my room, crouched down and, as I watched in amazement, pissed and took a shit at the same time.

It still smells a bit in that part of the room now. I don't know if it was the beer or country dancing that caused the problem – but I'm inclined to think the latter.

ACID INDIGESTION

*M*y older brother took me under his wing when I first went to university in London. I was an eighteen-year-old student dead keen to lose all of my naivety as quickly as possible. So I was naturally delighted when he took me to the best parties and introduced me to his cool older friends. The nicest thing out of all the lovely things that he did for me, however, was to take me out for a meal once a week to make sure I was eating OK. The only thing I'm not grateful for is the time when he was away on business and suggested that Jules, one of his friends, feed me that week instead.

'Don't worry,' my brother had said. 'He's a lovely guy, and anyway I've warned him to keep his hands off you. He's lots of fun, in a crazy kind of way, and he's stinking rich too. Probably take you somewhere far better than I can afford.'

That much was true at least. When Jules phoned up, he told me he'd booked us a table at 'a great little place I know in South Ken' (which turned out to be one of the swankiest restaurants in London at the time). He also said not to worry about getting there, as he'd come round to my hall of residence beforehand with 'the motor'.

When Jules arrived at my door, I discovered what my brother meant by 'fun in a crazy kind of way'. He produced a huge Camberwell Carrot from his pocket, explaining that his friend Harry had just picked up some 'simply killer weed' from 'the Dam' and I just had to try it.

Soon we were roaring with laughter in the back of the car – a top-of-the-range Jaguar, which I was relieved to note (given our state of intoxication) was chauffer-driven. When Jules suggested that we 'neck a bit of acid', I told myself I was in for one of the most amusing evenings of my life.

At first my predictions came true. Sitting in an incredibly posh room, drinking champagne, being waited on hand and foot and slurping my *potage aux légumes* noisily, while slowly getting more and more wasted on the LSD, tickled me so much that tears were rolling down my cheeks.

However, when I shared my delight in this mad juxtaposition of drug-based hedonism and high society with Jules, his face collapsed. 'My God,' he said anxiously. 'You don't think they're all looking at us do you?'

Suddenly everything took a turn for the worse. Everywhere I looked in the restaurant I saw staring eyes and disapproving faces. Sometimes five eyes per face. Sometimes more. I was losing my grip! Jules let out a small moan and stared down at his plate.

There was a bleak period when we both said nothing and concentrated furiously on trying to eat our food and appear normal. Then, after we'd struggled through our starters, Jules broke the silence.

'Pardon me,' he said. 'I'm terribly sorry, but I'm Satan. I'm the Devil, Prince of Darkness, and all the evil in the world is flowing out of me. I'm so very sorry.'

He started to stuff a napkin into his mouth, I presume to stem this flow of evil. A few minutes earlier, or any other time, I'd have been horribly embarrassed by his actions. Now, however, I was far too interested by the fly that was slowly drowning in my champagne glass. It seemed to tell me something about the futility of existence . . . I was obsessed . . . Then I realized that the fly wasn't there at all. I blinked, and fireworks exploded in my head.

From then on the evening went from bad to worse. I don't know how we managed to get through the rest of the meal, or how Jules managed to pay the bill, but I do know that he fell flat on his face as we made our way to the exit and had to be helped into the back of his Jaguar by the sommelier.

RED FACES ALL ROUND

*A*s often happens when things go terribly wrong, this night started off really well. I even thought that it could well have been the start of something special.

I'd met my new feller according to plan, and we'd gone for a relaxing drink or two. He'd paid me loads of attention and kept me laughing for ages, so I didn't hesitate when he suggested that we went clubbing. But as the night wore on, I got increasingly hammered. So drunk, in fact, that I couldn't find my bloke anywhere – and my temper got worse and worse.

'Sod it,' I eventually thought, after an age of wandering blearily and hopelessly round the dance floor, 'I'm going home.' But then, in the queue for the cloakroom, I met this really cute guy. One thing led to another, and he ended up going home with me.

I hadn't really expected to go far with him as I was on my period, but when the lights went out and I started feeling more and more horny and he offered to go down on me I was too befuddled to say anything. I just thought that I couldn't say no, not when the chance had been offered, and I lay back to enjoy myself. He didn't seem to mind either, not saying a word but putting in some damn good work.

Afterwards he got up to go to the loo. I heard a scream. I staggered out of bed to see what the problem was, but he was already pulling on his clothes and on his way out of the flat, shouting some-thing about how he had to go because his Mum would have been wondering where he'd gone. Seeing as he was twenty-five at the time, I didn't really believe him.

THE POO SOCK

James, an old friend of mine from university, liked the odd pint. When he went to meet his girlfriend's parents for the first time, the date involved staying overnight. Upon arrival they were shown to separate rooms, and James's girlfriend made it clear that her parents would not be happy with any attempts from him to creep around to see her after dark. So, whenever her father offered him another glass of beer, wine, single malt etc. (which was often), James had no hesitation in accepting.

Later that night, in the very early hours, he woke up. He was desperate for a crap. Tiptoeing out of the room, he found, to his horror, that he had absolutely no recollection which door led to the bathroom.

He was well aware that he was still very drunk. He was also unable to remember going to bed – so thought perhaps he hadn't acquitted himself all that well at the end of the evening. He didn't want to blot his copybook any further, but if he went into the parental bedroom by mistake, there was a good chance that he could wake them up and severely annoy them. Meanwhile, if he went into his girlfriend's room, they might not think it was a mistake. So he made a decision.

A few moments later James was back in his room. His trousers were round his ankles, and he was squatting. Over a sock. Which he was holding open with his hands. When he had finished this part of the operation, he began the second, even less advisable stage. Moving to the window, he opened it a little and leaned out. He swung the laden sock to propel it as far from the house as possible and let go. Then he went back to bed.

Some time later he woke up again. It was still ridiculously early, and, again nobody else was up. As he gradually came to, James realized just how lucky this was. There was shit everywhere. Carpet, walls, ceiling, curtains, furnishings, bedspread – almost nothing had escaped the shower of beery squits that his fantastic plan had unleashed.

Any net curtain-twitchers awake at that hour might have caught a brief glimpse of a sweaty, red-faced man gasping for breath as he belted down the road away from the house where he had been staying – and away from his then girlfriend – for ever. Had the Poo Police ever called at such a witness's house, and asked if the fleeing culprit had any distinguishing features, they might – had they been particularly eagle-eyed – have said, 'He was only wearing one sock, you know.'

A HEATED EXCHANGE

*A*t school I had a mate who was blessed with Mick Hucknall syndrome. That's to say: none of us thought he was good-looking, funny or charismatic, but he still somehow had the most incredible ability to attract women. Such was his obscene luck, in fact, that my other friends and I found him intensely annoying company if he ever accompanied us when we were out on the pull.

One night the table next to us was suddenly occupied by the most attractive girl any of us had ever seen within a 20-mile radius of the nightmare of hard, ugly, grey concrete (and even harder and uglier grey-faced locals) that passed for the centre of our home town. She was alone and, as our mate was already explaining with irritating confidence, ripe for the taking.

Even he was looking slightly nervous, however, and it wasn't until he'd had a couple more drinks that he plucked up the courage to walk over to her. We groaned inwardly, mentally preparing ourselves for the horrible sight of them leaving the pub arm in arm.

She looked up, smiled a lovely smile, and then he said, 'Hello, I'm your ex-husband.' 'Fuck off,' she immediately replied.

He was completely unable to explain his remarks.

GOING SOUTH

*A*fter sixth form I was working at a Foster's-for-under-£2 kind of pub, full of heavy-drinking misfits. One of the regulars was a South African, Rita – a big-boned, big-boobed blonde who was sexy from sixty yards if slightly less alluring close up, thanks to a skin made leathery by that South African sun.

One night Rita cajoled my co-worker Jane, a slightly bi-polar opera singer (who had to pull pints in the pub as she couldn't get work on the stage), and me along to an after-hours party at the flat of a scuzzy South African who had guzzled too much booze and swallowed too many drugs in his fifty-odd years.

The party was in full swing when we arrived, with all the local faces getting stuck into unbranded vodka and chain-smoking bootleg from Calais. I foolishly got drunk too and ended up snogging Rita. A few smutty cheers of the damned went up from the grubby throng in the kitchen.

Eventually Rita and I stumbled uninvited into the bedroom of our host. No sooner were we naked than the door swung open and the light was switched on blindingly. I clutched at the duvet to try, unsuccessfully, to preserve our modesty. Bold as brass, the host marched in and started rummaging in a bedside table while I sat up – astride Rita, who had decided to play dead rather than appeal to his sense of decency and ask him to leave.

I was mumbling my displeasure as my host roguishly slapped my naked arse. He asked: 'Are you having a good time there mate? Looks like you're having a real good time.' I decided enough was enough. 'Look, can you just fuck off?' I asked.

He flipped out. He slapped me harder and started shouting menacingly. 'YOU DON'T TELL ME TO FUCK OFF. THIS IS MY BEDROOM. YOU HEAR? I CAN COME AND GO AS I PLEASE . . .'

Etc.

To compound the nightmarish situation, I could see Rita's burly Afrikaans brother blocking out the doorway behind me. He grinned when I looked at him and explained that our host was just looking for condoms for him so he could 'have a good time' with another reveller, a lady-drunk of some fifty years (which made her at least twenty older than the brother).

Eventually I managed to placate the host, who left us to it. After a few shaming minutes of 'failing to recapture the mood' we got dressed and slinked out of the room, with me hoping to get away as quickly as possible.

However, there was no reprieve yet: Jane the opera singer had been visited by the black dog of depression. Possibly she felt excluded from all the 'good times' being had. She stared catatonically into the middle distance. Rita decided she wasn't going to leave her in this state, and I, having agreed to walk Rita home, was forced to sit there playing along with the lewd banter of the drunks for – and I do not exaggerate – two more hours.

TRIVIA

DOOMED LOVE: HELOISE AND ABELARD

Heloise and Abelard were perfect for each other. He was a rising member of the all-powerful clergy, the greatest logical philosopher of his generation and something of a heart-throb in twelfth-century Paris. She was a beautiful and fiercely intelligent young woman, living in the care of one the most important men in the city, the Canon of Notre-Dame Cathedral – her loving Uncle Fulbert.

So when Abelard met Heloise in 1115, he was immediately smitten. Cashing in on his reputation as one of the best teachers around, and knowing Fulbert's love of money, Abelard suggested to the uncle that he became a paying lodger in his house and tutor Heloise. His plan worked admirably. Abelard took up residence, Heloise proved a willing pupil, and he was soon teaching her far more than dry logic. 'My hands strayed more often over the curves of her body than to the pages,' he remembered happily in his autobiographical account of their love. 'Our desires left no stage of love making untried, and if love could devise something new, we welcomed it.'

Less welcome, however, was the intrusion of Uncle Fulbert, who several months into the affair caught the couple when they were hard at it.

An elopement, a baby and a secret marriage later Uncle Fulbert was eager for revenge. He broke into Abelard's new lodgings with some friends, where Abelard himself describes what happened: 'They cut off the parts of my body whereby I had committed the wrong of which they complained.' In short, they castrated the poor man.

BAD PLANNING

*M*y best friend had just been invited to meet her boyfriend's parents. She was ever so nervous. She was especially worried about meeting his mum, who she'd heard was a fiercely intelligent and staunchly conservative doctor. Fortunately the meeting went well.

Relieved and happy, she decided that now she and the boyfriend were getting so serious, it was time to go on some more stable form of contraception. She rocked up to the family planning clinic the next morning and walked straight in to see . . . his mum!

DATE . . . OF BIRTH

I saw a girl sitting in a café. She was a little bit older than me, but very pretty and glowing all the same. When her female friend had gone to settle the bill, I sidled over and started chatting to her. After a debonair compliment, I asked her if she would like to have lunch some time. She said yes and then laughed. When I asked why, she steadied herself and stood up. She was *very* pregnant. She pointed at her stomach and asked, 'You wouldn't have a problem with this?'

Not wanting to seem like a churlish philistine of the pre-PC era and, perhaps a little curious, even turned on by the thought of dating a pregnant woman, I said that as long as the father didn't mind, I didn't mind.

A few days later our lunch date came around, I had picked out my favourite curry house in Bristol. She showed up on time and we were getting along fine. When the food arrived, I decided to hit the Gents for a slash and to wash my hands. When I came back, I noticed that her face had turned a little white. I asked if everything was OK. She shook her head and pointed under the table. I didn't need to look to realize her waters had broken.

She asked: 'Will you take me to the hospital?' Which I did, in a taxi, after calmly paying the bill while she sat puppy-like above a pool of her own fluid. I left her at the hospital after phoning a very suspicious mother and beckoning her to the maternity wing.

A day later I did pop in and see her with the new man in her life, who had arrived safe and sound, in spite of being so premature. She asked me if I had been back to the curry house to apologize for the mess she had made. I hadn't and she joked, to her credit, that Mothercare gave you free nappies for a year if your waters break in there . . . and she was wondering if she could perhaps rely on free lamb bhunas in the future.

KEEPING MUM

*M*ark B. was one of the coolest lads at the local boys' grammar school. Handsome, clever, shy, quiet, sober, crisply dressed and ever so slightly – and alluringly – sardonic. Which is why it was such a shock meeting his mother.

She was a fright: all long greying hair, giant purple skirt, tie-dyed T-shirt and screams of delight as she rushed out of the car to meet me – half elbowing her son off my doorstep in the process.

As I was wrapped in her warm and far too fragrant embrace it came as even more of a shock to be told that she fully intended to accompany Mark and me on our forthcoming trip to see *Terminator* 2. She was, she said, anxious not to miss the sight of her son's first love blossoming.

My mild protests were wafted aside in a breeze of incense and patchouli, and I soon found myself sitting in the back of her 2CV next to a mortified-looking Mark. He looked mortified because his mum was enthusiastically and graphically explaining the facts of life to me. She had to, she'd said. 'Mark already knows all about it, of course, but I'm aware that other parents are afraid of passing on these kinds of details. But you must find out before it's too late. Now. Do you know how to put a condom on?'

This was more than my nervous, virginal, fourteen-year-old brain could cope with coming from an oldster, and the rest of the journey passed in a haze of horror and embarrassment. Mercifully,

Mrs B. elected to stay in the car while we watched the film. I remember this being rather dull in itself, but a terrifically exciting experience nonetheless as Mark held my hand all the way through it.

But the romance was quickly extinguished when we got outside and Mrs B. asked her son if he'd snogged me yet. Mark just smiled sweetly and told her to piss off. Even then she remained alarmingly happy, smiling beatifically and pontificating on how strong and protective her son had grown and what a beautiful experience she was sharing.

Mark said goodbye to me on my doorstep with Mrs B. looking on and beaming encouragement from the front seat of the car all the while. 'I'm sorry about Mum,' he whispered. 'I had to let her come. I just couldn't bear to hurt her feelings . . .'

It was then that I got a funny feeling in my stomach alarmingly like the one Mrs B. had just been describing on the hellish ride home.

Over the next couple of years, when Mark and I went out together, I even got to like Mrs B. a lot too: although I always drew the line at letting her tell my fortune, and never ever allowed her to feed me one of her 'special' cakes.

COITUS INTERRUPTUS

*M*y boyfriend and I were determined to lose our virginity. Both our respective parents were determined that we should keep it. His were especially insistent, their innate conservatism backed up by religious fervour and (I suspect) mild insanity on the part of his mother. Since it was small-town America, quite a few years ago, the old folks were winning our battle of wills.

Already they'd done everything they could to break us apart, short of locking us in our rooms. Naturally, this just made us more determined and more desperate, not least because, if there was one thing we'd both inherited from our folks, it was stubbornness.

Since our parents had insisted that we didn't go out together unsupervised, we decided that the only thing for it was to do the deed in his house. The idea was that if we went in his old-fashioned shower, its wheezing and spluttering would hide any of our own noises.

The big day arrived. Everyone else was downstairs preparing supper (thereby giving a good reason why one of us might be having a wash), the shower was spluttering away lustily, we were lustily spluttering and all of a sudden we lost our balance and crashed to the floor. To make matters worse, my boyfriend tried to grab hold of the shower to steady himself and pulled that down with him too, wrenching the unit from the wall with a terrific ripping and banging noise.

Luckily we weren't hurt, but unluckily (it being that kind of household) there was no lock on the door, and the next thing we knew his mum was running in screaming that I was a slut and yelling about the fires in hell that were just waiting for me. I barely had time to dress before I was thrown out.

Funnily enough, her husband left her six months later, when he discovered that she'd been having an affair with a local preacher. Just goes to show!

TRIVIA

FUNNY OLD WORLD: BUNDLING

Puritan parents in seventeenth-century America used to believe that true love was the firmest foundation for marriage. They thought that one of the best tests of this love was to see how well a prospective couple would get on after a night in the same bed. They did not, however, believe in premarital sex. In case the pair got on too well, God-fearing parents used to put a great big piece of wood – known as the bundling board – in the bed between them. The luckless female child's legs were also wrapped securely in a 'bundling stocking'.

Naturally, in spite of these precautions, the custom of bundling is known to have resulted in many premarital pregnancies.

A HEAVY PRICE

On our first night out I'd mentioned in passing that I liked a drop of full cream milk in my coffee. So on our second date I was touched when we went back to his, he offered me coffee and he told me he'd laid in some of the old blue-top milk. Very nice . . . or so I thought until it came to time to leave and he said, 'Oh and I paid 30p for that milk – but you can have what's left for 25.'

UNBEARABLE

*J*oe is one of my favourite people. We'd been on a few dates when this happened, and had learned some of each other's quirks. He only liked real ales and had a bear costume; I'm interested in the poet Yeats but hadn't known how to pronounce his name until I was – to my horror – corrected at a university interview. We were just starting out in the happy game of dating.

Picture a Friday night after a long day at work. Joe's coming to pick me up from a business drink with a colleague from a magazine company. He rings in the afternoon to check what time to come and places great emphasis on the idea that he only wants to arrive after the business types have left. I say come for seven.

We're sitting in the bar, and the business types are still there at 7.15. I wonder where Joe is. My PA is sitting beside me, and leans over and laughs into my ear: 'I think I'm on drugs . . . a seven-foot bear just came in!'

My blood freezes. I look around the table at the people I've just been acting all suave with. Then I turn my head to confront what can only be a 6 foot 2 inch man in a bear costume . . . which makes him into a giant. The bear is in some state of distress, as am I.

He comes over to hug me with his bag full of the groceries he's bought to make me dinner later. But – curse my hard heart – I'm nothing but embarrassed. Not charmed at all. I actually just want to sink into the earth and die. My friends and colleagues, however, are all mightily impressed and absolutely creased up with laughter. My PA particularly is raining charming blonde chortles upon all of us. I think she cried she was laughing so much.

Anyway, the bear is thirsty. (Apparently the bear suit is hot.) He goes to get some water, which he drinks (admittedly quite cutely) while clutching the glass with both paws.

All this time my business types are sitting there too, observing a section of my now not-very-private life. So the bear is dispatched home, and I finish up the meeting. Everyone keeps busting into laughter every few minutes and agreeing that it's an amazing thing for anyone to do.

Unfortunately, I didn't see it that way. I was just embarrassed. I let bear guy go.

POSTSCRIPT

Fortunately, this story has a happy ending. A year or so later I realized that I had pretty fond memories of Joe, and that I wondered how he was doing. I took him out for dinner and a penguin movie to celebrate getting a merit in his Master's degree and, to cut a long story short, I've never felt quite like this about anyone before.

Think about it: how much character, confidence and simple joy in life does it take to wear a bear costume and take the Underground across London to charm a girl?

THE DEVIL IN ME

*I*t was my friend Paul who persuaded me to have a go at internet dating. I was young, single and hopelessly sex-starved at the time, and during a session of Sunday afternoon drinking in the pub he had told me about his new girlfriend. He'd met her on-line and – contrary to my internet dating prejudices and preconceptions – she was pretty, petite, educated (a professional opera singer, no less) and a knock-out in bed. This wasn't just bravado on Paul's part, either. According to his housemate, who was also with us and who had the room beneath Paul, she climaxed extremely loudly and just couldn't seem to get enough of it. Crass, I know, but that swung it. I thought, why not?

In fact, I was so impressed by Paul's newfound happiness that I decided to have a go at it the very next day. This also happened to be the first day of my new job, and when my line manager – who was supposed to be settling me in – disappeared for a meeting and I found myself with absolutely nothing to do, I clicked onto Google and typed in 'singles'. Needless to say, a plethora of sites sprang up. There was something for everyone, it seemed – but try as I might, I just couldn't feel enthused.

I mean, what did you do? How did you decide what to write? And what did they mean, 'Be sincere'? Did they mean honest? I didn't think the truth would get me very far: 'M, 25, 5′ 9″, up to his ears in student debt, with barely passable looks – and absolutely desperate for a shag. With anyone.'

I just couldn't do it. And I couldn't lie either. After all, how would I ever recover from the look of disappointment on the poor girl's face when she realized that she wasn't about to spend an evening with a Nobel laureate and Brad Pitt lookalike?

There was one thing that I could do, however, even if I wasn't, after all that, going to bag myself a gorgeous sexpot soprano. And that was have a laugh. See, the thing was that in among all of those 'normal' dating sites, I'd spotted another one. This was a Christian site, with free membership to all of those singles who 'already have one man in their life – Jesus'.

I thought I'd place an ad there. 'LUCIFER (M, 7′11″ WGSOH) WLTM female with plenty of soul to make the beast with two backs, spend long nights in front of the hot fires of hell and do naughty things with pitchforks.'

Well, I thought it was funny. They didn't, though.

I'd completely forgotten about the whole thing when I was called into the office of my new company's Human Resources witch. She sat me down with the office techie, who explained that he'd been getting some 'complaints'. Basically, the Christian website owners had traced the IP from my message back to my office's server. Then the office computer man read back my advert, which really didn't sound as amusing in his thick Scottish accent – and under those personally trying circumstances (although I suspect he was quite enjoying himself). My laughter levels did not increase any when the HR woman told me that I'd nearly blown my probation, and if I did anything like that again she'd 'unfortunately' have to take rather more drastic action than giving me a verbal warning.

So, that was the end of my short life as Satan and, alas, my internet dating career.

TRIVIA

BEYOND BELIEF: LOT AND HIS WIFE

The Bible says that Lot's marriage was brought to an unexpected and tragic end when God turned Lot's wife into a pillar of salt. God did this because she'd disobeyed a specific order. He'd allowed the star-crossed couple to escape from the city of Sodom before he rained fire and brimstone down on it, but told them both not to look back. Lot's wife couldn't resist, and that was the end of her.

Afterwards Lot went to live in a cave and slept with both of his daughters. God didn't seem to mind about that.

A BIG QUESTION

I thought it had been a tolerable evening. Not exactly sparkling, but there was certainly room for further exploration. So at the end of the date I asked: 'Do you want to meet again?'

'What on earth for?' he replied.

NOT-SO-HARD HARD MAN

I'd made contact after seeing his details in the Lonely Hearts column of the local newspaper: a man with twenty-two years in the armed forces. Just what I needed. What a man, I thought. He just had to be macho with a record like that. Better yet, when we spoke on the phone he sounded nice. A heart of gold, and biceps made of iron . . . I spent a long time daydreaming about him before we met.

We hooked up in a local pub, and everything went well for the first ten minutes, helped along by his rugged good looks and an iron-man physique clearly visible beneath his tight T-shirt. What a man, I thought again. Then came the bombshell.

'I have a problem,' he said. 'I've been impotent for quite a while. But I have got hold of some Viagra pills and wondered if you would help me see if they work? There's a little B&B near by which I've booked and . . . and I hope we can do the business.'

Now, either he was using just about the worst routine ever invented by the male species on me – and he was therefore a real sleaze – or my iron man actually had a consistency more like a jelly-filled balloon in a rather vital area. Either way, I was speechless.

COKE HEAD ACHE

*T*his was actually a date that went so well it turned into a disaster. Being young and not knowing quite as much about South American politics as I do now, I'd taken quite a lot of 'naughty salts' with my then boyfriend. Then we'd gone back to his for what I was keenly anticipating would be a marathon sex session.

It was, I can safely say, the best sex I've had. So good, in fact, that as I reached orgasm, I flung my head back in ecstasy – and trapped a nerve in my neck. My cry of delight quickly turned to a scream of pain, and I discovered that not only was I in complete agony but I couldn't move my head to left or right.

My boyfriend had to prize me into my clothes, lever me into his car and take me down to casualty, where I had the horrifically embarrassing task of explaining what had happened to a young, male and alarmingly handsome doctor. He was very professional and didn't laugh, but I could see a tell-tale sparkle in his eye when he explained how cocaine and sex can both contract blood vessels and that with my sudden head movement this had made it easier for me to trap a nerve, that this had gone into spasm . . . and that I was going to have to wear a collar and have intensive physiotherapy for the next two weeks. 'And don't', he said, 'try anything too acrobatic for a while, either.'

TRIVIA

LOVE HURTS: SURVEYING THE DAMAGE

Over-enthusiastically shagging British couples cause £350 million damage each year, according to a survey by adult chain store Ann Summers. A third of couples said that they had broken something during sex, and 10 per cent had even made insurance claims. Damaged items include lamps, vases and beds and even pulled-down curtains.

Meanwhile, it wasn't just inanimate objects they were damaging. An impressive 41 per cent of respondents said that they had suffered carpet burns, a third suffered from pulled backs and 12 per cent twisted ankles or wrists. Other injuries in the Top Ten list were (in descending order of frequency) twisted ankles, bruised bottoms, bruised legs, grazed elbows, scratched backs, bumped heads and broken bones.

Couples in the south-east were the most accident-prone, while Yorkshire lovers put in the most claims for damage.

DRUGS DON'T WORK

*M*uch to all our friends' dismay, Joe and I had been on about thirty dates in less than nine months but had had no physical contact. I tried all the tricks, but nothing seemed to be working. He still hadn't kissed me. I was told by a mutual friend that he was just shy and did like me a lot, so I persevered, but I was beginning to wonder if we would ever have a future.

Anyway, not too long ago I had been invited to a thirtieth birthday meal, and I asked Joe along as my date. Catastrophically (as it turned out), I was really unwell on the day with what I later found to be an inflamed tooth nerve and an ear infection. I probably should have called Joe and my friends and cancelled, but I was so desperate to see Joe and show him off to my friends that I decided to go ahead.

To get me through the night, I had been popping a combination of Co-codamol and Ibuprofen tablets to try and dull the pain, but nothing was working. I also hadn't eaten for over twenty-four hours, as it was too painful to chew. I decided that alcohol would have to be my last resort.

It was a bad idea.

As soon as the smallest bit of food hit my stomach, it reacted with the cocktail of legal drugs and alcohol. I had to rush to the Ladies and was violently sick. I then came back downstairs to resume the evening as though nothing had happened, but the date devil was against me and I then fainted at the dinner table . . .

I didn't even manage to fall into Joe's arms, just kind of slumped into my chair.

A TOUGH CALL

I didn't really know my prospective romance partner, and I knew I didn't want to know him when, within five minutes of our first (and last) arranged meeting, he took a call on his mobile phone. This, of course, was rude enough, but it was the fact that he started yelling at the person on the other end of the line that really alarmed me. I've pretty much erased what he said from my mind, but I can't forget the moment when he told his caller that he wished he'd run her over when he had the chance.

'Sorry,' he said, when he finally got off the phone. He smiled ingratiatingly. 'Women, eh?' he said. 'That was my awful ex-wife. Drives me mental. I can't stand to talk to her. I hope you aren't going to be a cow like her.'

I told him that the only thing I was going was away – and ran for the nearest taxi.

TRIVIA

FUNNY OLD WORLD: OUT OF HIS TREE

Gayadhar Parida, an octogenarian from Orissa in India, has spent more than fifty years up a mango tree after a row with his wife. The quarrel was over a 'tiny issue', according to the *Mumbai Mirror*, but Mr Parida has never moved back home.

He did change residence once, when his original tree was blown down in a storm, but otherwise he descends only to drink water from a pool. He is fed by family members but refuses absolutely to come down from his perch. His son Babula explained: 'I have gone to the garden several times to woo him back, but he vehemently refused to return. Hurt and dejected, I had to come back home.'

CREATING THE WRONG IMPRESSION

I went out to a club with some mates. Having been dumped just recently, I got tanked up on cheap alcopops and hit the dance floor. I spotted a tall, nice-looking guy over the other side of the room and flashed him a bright, though drunken, smile.

The evening drew on and about 2 a.m., having made no real progress, my friends all decided to head back home. By this stage I'd lost sight of my man. My mates went to fetch coats, and I headed out of the club to get some fresh air and wait for them. To my surprise I noticed the fit guy leaning against a wall on the other side of the road. He came over and started chatting. By the time my friends came out, he had invited me back to his place and I'd agreed.

We had a brilliant night, and that got me back to feeling on top form. But the next morning, when I woke up, he was nowhere to be found. Since the house was empty, I got dressed and went to leave. Just as I went to let myself out, I noticed a wad of cash in the top of my handbag.

I stared. I took the money. I vowed never to wear such a short skirt again.

TRIVIA

FUNNY OLD WORLD: X-RATED MOVIE MAN

In April 2006 Kevin Costner was accused of mistaking a masseuse for a prostitute. The incident was said to have taken place when the Hollywood star was on his honeymoon in St Andrews in 2004. The masseuse claimed that Costner asked her if she'd be 'comfortable' touching him 'everywhere'. She said that she replied in the negative, whereupon the actor started making furtive movements under his towel. Moments later he 'whipped off' all coverings and 'exposed himself', performing a lewd act of self-dating.

BYE, POLES, DISORDER

*T*he evening was already pretty much ruined in my book when, rather than accompanying me to my work party as we'd planned, my girlfriend dumped me. And as it turned out, that was just a prelude to the horrors to come. The party was a barbecue in the back garden of a house in Putney, owned by one of the Polish builders my architectural company had just finished working with.

Polish builders like vodka. They like to share their vodka. I was feeling morose. I wanted to drink their vodka. It was very strong. Too strong . . . This was a lethal equation.

At first I thought I was going to enjoy myself. I couldn't understand the words of the songs we were singing, but roaring along with my smiling new friends was good. Good too was the fact that the buxom daughter of the other guests was smiling in a special way at me.

Even better was the moment when she grabbed me on my way back from the bathroom and started to snog me.

Events started to spiral out of control, however, when a work colleague tapped me on the back, extricated me from the embrace and whispered in my ear that the girl was only fifteen – and it would probably be a good idea for me to leave the party RIGHT AWAY.

Now, the thing I've noticed about drinking extremely strong spirits is that it takes a little while for the effects of all the alcohol to hit you. I'd thought I was merely damn drunk – but by the time

I'd made a clumsy dash for the street I realized that actually I was only one step away from catatonic.

And that's why I wasn't particularly surprised when I came to in Walthamstow, where a taxi driver was screaming at me to 'get the fuck out' of his cab. Although I was very confused. I live in Hackney, and there was really no good reason for me to be in E17 at all. I really couldn't understand why I was there.

All such philosophical musings were interrupted, however, when the driver grabbed my arm and yanked me physically from the seat. I lay on the ground where he'd left me, looking up at the stars – and the blue trousers of the policeman leaning over me. In fact, there was a whole bevy of policemen there. And a van. God knows why.

'Are you all right there?' one of them was asking.

The sensible thing to have done then would have been to reply in the affirmative and walk off quietly. So I said 'No!' Then I explained that I was 'fucking lost' and asked him would he give me some directions. Or maybe a lift in his van?

'I think it's time to go home. You've had enough excitement for one evening.'

I wasn't going to take that. It was dangerous in Walthamstow, and I didn't know the way home anyway. I decided that the safest course would be to try to get myself arrested, so that I could spend the night inside, safely locked away from all the perils the outside world presented to my inebriated self.

So I started trying to call the gathered police people 'pigs', 'wankers', 'fascists'. I think my shame is compounded by the fact that they just ignored me. Then the scene blurs in my mind.

The rest of my exchange with the policemen – if anything else at all was said – has faded from my memory. As has everything else, in fact, until I woke up the following morning with a screaming headache and a pressing urge to be sick. I also had blisters on my feet and cuts on my knees, which lead me to wonder to this day whether, in the end, I crawled home.

Later on that afternoon I realized that I'd acquired the (young) girl's number and tried to call her so she could fill in the blanks in my memory. She never answered.

NOT CHICKEN (I)

We were both drunk. I could tell by the way we were both standing in a fried chicken restaurant in Hackney. I'd never have gone there if I were sober. Never. The way I was cackling too: that also suggested I was definitely too many pints down the line. I really was laughing insanely. That was a very bad sign.

The strongest indication of our inebriation, however, was the way the girl I was with was point-blank demanding that the guys behind the counter let her use their (non-customer) toilet and threatening that if they didn't, she'd have to 'wazz' all over the floor.

Those familiar with Hackney will know that this kind of behaviour is not a good idea. Drawing attention to yourself once the sun's set in that part of town is not a safe course of action.

The Fear finally penetrated my happy alcoholic haze when I became aware of the muttering in the queue behind me. This fear rapidly turned to terror when my date proceeded to climb up on to the counter of the chicken shack, started dancing and announced that the staff and everyone in the place were a 'bunch of fucking wankers' and that she wasn't going to let anyone get their food until she'd been allowed to micturate.

Nothing I could say would bring her down, and the vibes were getting ever more hostile. A large man in the queue was muttering and swearing. When he called the girl a bitch, I thought I ought to try and diffuse the situation. Naturally, that only made things worse.

'I can't hit a girl mate, – and I would hit you for bringing that tart here, but I can't hit a man wearing glasses either.'

I tried to ask him not to call her a tart. And then, rather foolishly, I added an insult of my own. He pulled my glasses off my face, screwed them up in his huge hands and threw them out the door of the shop into the road.

'I suppose you're going to hit me in the face now, dickhead?' I asked, again rather foolishly.

The next thing I knew, I was picking myself up off the floor. Luckily, drunk as I was, it didn't really hurt, and it at least persuaded my female friend to come down off the counter. I suffered no more lasting damage than the humiliation of having to appear at work the next day with the frame of my glasses sellotaped together. Looking even further on the bright side, I'd proved that I wasn't chicken.

TRIVIA

BEASTLY HABITS: PENIS FENCING

Like humans, animals often fight over their mates. Male elephants will fight for hours, uprooting trees and throwing logs at each other in the process. The battle often goes on to the death. If there is a clear winner before this extreme is reached, he chases the loser for several miles before ceasing hostilities.

More unusual is the mating ritual of *Pseudobiceros hancockanus*. This is a hermaphrodite species of flatworm. The worm's penis has a sharp tip with which the worm tries to pierce the skin of its potential mate – who is also trying to do the same thing to him/her. These penis duels can last up to an hour. The winner gets to transfer its sperm. The loser has to take on the burden of motherhood.

A RELATIONSHIP BREAKDOWN

I accepted a date with an Italian surgeon. It was a silly thing to do. I was in the middle of studying for some important exams. Every hour of my time counted, and I really had none to spare.

But you kind of have to accept that sort of date, don't you? I mean: a) he was a surgeon; and b) I knew he had an awesome car, a BMW Z4 convertible. And I'd never been in a convertible before – let alone with a hot Italian doctor.

It was great when he purred up my drive in the flashy motor to pick me up. I felt like quite a princess. Not so great was his rather panicky announcement two minutes later that he was about to run out of petrol and that he needed to know – right away – where the nearest petrol station was.

I directed him to the ring road, where I knew there was a super-market selling petrol. Fourth exit at the roundabout, I told him. So he took the second, and we started speeding off on the wrong side of the ring road, getting further from the fuel we desperately needed at 70 m.p.h.

After about a mile the car predictably churned to a grinding halt. We just about managed to push it into a lay-by and then had to run across the dual carriageway, tramp across several muddy fields to the petrol station, buy two litre bottles of water, empty them, fill them up with petrol (trying not to spill it on our clothes and hands), walk all the way back, fill the tank, then drive the car all the way around the ring road to the petrol station . . .

In short, not much fun.

When we finally got back on to the road, my hour was most definitely up. I didn't feel or look at all like a princess any more, and I was utterly convinced I was never going to let that particular surgeon operate on me!

TRIVIA

BEYOND BELIEF: A FAMILY AFFAIR

As well as singing about cars, Dennis Wilson of the Beach Boys was expert at picking up girls in them. He bit off more than he could chew, however, when he picked up two followers of the infamous Charles Manson, the bearded anti-hippy whose cult The Family killed the pregnant film star Sharon Tate.

At first, Wilson got on well with the girls – and with Manson, who was able to supply him with yet more nubile young females. He even persuaded his famous band to record one of Manson's compositions, 'Learn Not To Love'. But when Manson and The Family moved into Wilson's house, things quickly got out of hand. By the time the Beach Boy managed to evict them, he estimated that they'd cost him more than $100,000. He had to pay for the Mercedes they'd smashed up, a round of gonorrhoea injections and the fact that they helped themselves to wads of cash. The final straw came, however, when Charlie threatened the nervous Dennis by waving a bullet at one of his friends, claiming it was a message and making dark hints about where it might end up.

MAKING A MEAL OF THINGS

I was staying in Cardiff while doing some work for my law firm and had decided to spend my £20 expenses allowance on getting some Chinese food from the restaurant near my hotel. But I was feeling distinctly uncomfortable. The restaurant was extremely cramped, and I'd been placed at a table in such a way that I was almost in the laps of a couple who were clearly there on a romantic night out. They'd ordered huge plates full of seafood, including lobster, were already tucking into champagne and were looking lovingly into each other's eyes.

The last thing they wanted was my face coming in between them, so I did my best to keep a low profile, paying particular attention to the menu and then the legal notes I had gathered up in front of me. It wasn't working, though. I felt sure that the woman was giving me dirty looks. Then, when she pulled her man over so she could whisper in his ear, I felt sure she was whispering about me.

'Look at him. What's he doing on his own? Staring at us . . .'

Did she really say that, I wondered? No, no. I decided I was just being paranoid. Then she started speaking louder, making sure I could hear this time.

'Why's he here on his own? Is he a weirdo?'

The man shushed her, obviously embarrassed, and smiled uncomfortably at me.

'Leave him alone. He's fine,' he said kindly. 'Just trying to have a meal now, isn't he.'

'He's staring at me I tell you! He's a weirdo! He's not even eating. What's he doing?'

I was actually trying my damnedest not to catch either of their eyes, hiding as best I could behind my papers and praying the waiter would come over soon, so I would at least have a plate of food between myself and this increasingly furious woman. The guy tried to calm her down again, but this made things worse.

'I'm not sitting here having him staring at us. I came here for a romantic meal with you, not you and some ginger weirdo.' To my horror she then started shouting.

'He's looking at my fucking breasts, isn't he!' she cried at a volume sure to attract the attention of every other diner in the place to my now glowing red face. This was the last straw for her partner, whom I was now definitely warming to.

'Now come on,' he said. 'You're out of order.'

'Out of order, am I? Well, I'll tell you what. Fuck you!'

'What?'

'Fuck you! I'm leaving.'

With that she picked up the keys that had been lying on the table and stormed off. The guy sat for a while looking shell-shocked. It was impossible for me not to catch his eye, since we were sitting cheek by jowl opposite each other.

'Women eh?' he sighed. 'Can't live with them. Can't live without them.'

I apologized, horribly embarrassed, saying I hoped I hadn't ruined their evening. 'Not at all, not at all. Wasn't your fault, was it?' he said, smiling in sympathy. And, then, before I knew it, I'd slid over on to the seat on his table and we were chatting and laughing, getting on like a house on fire. Suddenly all of the food the couple had ordered arrived. Great mounds of it.

'Look,' he pointed out. 'I've got all this food here now, no point letting it go to waste.'

So I started tucking in. He even poured me a glass of the champagne and soon had me screaming with laughter at tales of his other adventures with Gladys, whom he clearly loved, but who equally clearly gave him hell.

It was just as he was reaching the punchline of one of these hilarious stories and I was waving my arms in delighted animation – her glass of champagne in one hand, almost a whole lobster in another – that I noticed a presence. Positioned as we were, I could see her and he couldn't. But he soon noticed the look of horror on my face. He turned slowly.

'Hello there, my love.'

'Oh hello, darling. Don't let me interrupt,' she said, her face white, her voice now steady and quiet – and all the more menacing for it. 'After all, I only came back here to tell you that I love you. But you'd obviously rather talk to your new friend and give him my champagne and . . . OH FUCK YOU!'

And that was that. She stormed off again. I sidled back to my table, keen not to make things worse for my new friend, just in case she came back. I left shortly afterwards, feeling completely mortified and leaving him staring at the empty seat opposite.

SUNSET

I'd fancied James for months, but we were hardly ever alone. Apart from one drunken dalliance, ours was a case of an unrequited crush and missed opportunities – until the Notting Hill Carnival. As luck would have it, James and I were separated from the people we'd arrived with. We were both quite drunk, and it was a sunny afternoon, so instead of getting the Tube, we decided to walk back to my place in north-west London, where everyone else would meet us.

Emboldened by Red Stripe, I decided our walk would be 'it'. . . I could charm James with my one funny joke and then, aided by the setting sun, make my move.

All was going well until James stopped to tie his shoelace. Ducking down, he was momentarily distracted while I continued to walk past him, gazing in a slightly goofy manner at his lovely broad shoulders and missing a bloody great lamp-post, which, just in time, I managed to turn around and walk straight into, bearing most of the impact on the bridge of my nose.

I weebled for a second or two but remained upright and relatively OK. Until an avalanche of white-hot pain hit me, rendering me completely senseless.

Luckily, or so I thought, James had been completely distracted by his lace, as I gingerly inched round to face him. Standing up, he gave me a smile, which I reciprocated, before bursting into tears, partly through shock, partly through pain.

As the tears continued to stream down my cheeks, my metal-pranged brain was sending frantic messages: 'Recover the situation'; 'It's not too late'.

So, in between snot bubbles that a five-year-old would be proud of, I explained to the slightly alarmed object of my lust that I couldn't stop crying because of the beauty of the sunset. 'It's just soooo beeeewwwwwtiiiiiifullllll,' I gibbered, hiccupping as the crying wouldn't stop.

Smiling reassurance as several men walked past, James began rubbing the top part of my back. I then threw up on his shoes and felt much better.

To this day I have a dent in my nose I've never told anyone the provenance of – until now . . .

NOW YOU'RE STALKING

I'd been getting a lot of attention from a girl for quite a long while. She was a decent enough type. I liked her OK – but not in the way she wanted. I just didn't fancy her at all. I'd told her so too. But that hadn't deterred her from following me around. She even seemed to imagine we had some kind of relationship, which made me a bit nervous. My flat mates had started calling her The Stalker. They found it all very funny.

Somehow she found out about the party we were throwing, and I didn't have the heart to tell her not to come. Of course, as soon as she arrived, she started following me around. I did my very best to fend her off and concentrate on the fridge full of beer. She, however, wouldn't take no for an answer, and even before people had started to leave, she announced that she was tired and going to sleep in my bed (my room being the only one – as bad luck would have it – that wasn't full of people at the time).

I was too drunk to deal with the situation properly, especially since my attention had been distracted by a very pretty German girl. Once my 'stalker' was out of sight and out of mind, this girl and I were able to talk properly. And we talked for hours, getting steadily closer as the night wore on, ignoring everyone else around us. When my housemate came and asked if one of his friends could crash in my room, I just said, 'Yes, of course,' thinking 'Go away' and making nothing of it.

By 2 a.m. most of the guests had left, and the German girl and I were left in the sitting-room, increasingly frustrated that we didn't have a bed to go to. She kept asking why I didn't just throw everyone else out, but I knew I couldn't because the other girl was in there and I was sure that would just create a scene.

My phone had been going several times too, but I'd blithely ignored it. I'd also done nothing when I heard someone storming down the hallway and the front door slamming. In fact, I was falling asleep.

I was rudely awakened, far too early in the morning, when my stalker stormed into the room wanting to know: a) what the hell I was doing sleeping with my arms around this other girl; and b) why the hell I'd told another man to go and sleep with her.

It was then that I realized the horrible mistake I'd made. My stalker went on to explain that she'd been phoning me and phoning me to come and help her out, especially when the man in bed with her had suddenly started to try and cuddle her. Eventually she'd elbowed him hard in the nads – and he'd stormed off, which is why I'd heard the door slam in the middle of the night.

Worse was to follow, however, when my stalker and my German girl got talking and began deciding that the whole thing demonstrated absolutely despicable behaviour on my part. Not long afterwards they went out the house together, bosom buddies, leaving me alone, hung-over and sweating on the sofa.

TRIVIA

BEASTLY HABITS: STALKER SQUIRREL

Once a male Idaho ground squirrel has located a female mate, he never lets her out of his sight. He follows her everywhere she goes – and attacks any male squirrel that even comes near her.

A DESPERATE SITUATION

A couple of years ago I received an invitation to a party from an ex-girlfriend. At the time I was single and desperate for sex, so I thought this could be the answer. After all, why would she invite me in the first place? We hadn't spoken in months.

As with most of the ideas my brain seems to spew out, this nooky notion was to be proved completely wrong. It was an 'Engagement Party' – a little fact that my ex had neglected to mention, presumably so she could rub my face in it one last time. The worst of it all was that I had already asked her if I could crash over at her place.

Needless to say, I got heroically drunk and spent most of the night sat in a corner eating poorly baked 'party-time' sausage rolls and brooding. When the party was over, I was given a sleeping bag by the husband-to-be, who, I might add, had seemed to an alright bloke until half-way through the night when I decided that in fact he was a complete knobhead. This decision may have been booze-induced.

I set about going to sleep, so that I could get up and leave as early as possible the next morning. Unfortunately, half-way through, my bladder interrupted my blissful rest. I resisted the urge for as long as humanly possible, hoping to sleep on through until morning, but to no avail.

By the time I got to the bathroom door, I was absolutely bursting. But this door was half-open, and from the sounds emanating from within I guessed that the happy couple were in full shag.

Big problem. I could no longer wait and hurried back downstairs to find something to relieve myself in before I made a terrible mess of the floor.

The kitchen held the answer: a large yellow Tupperware jug. I let go. It was bliss – standing in the kitchen weeing into my ex-girlfriend's big plastic jug.

I awoke the next morning to find ex-girlfriend and husband-to-be were already up and about, ironing. Ironing with 'water' from the plastic jug.

He said, 'This water's been here overnight. Will it be OK?'

'Of course, you silly sausage,' she replied.

NOT CHICKEN (II)

A man approached me. 'You know you're just like KFC,' he said.

'What?'

'You know, big breasts, big thighs . . .'

I was confused – and not particularly amused. I asked him if he was trying to say that I was fat.

'No,' he said quickly. 'Don't you get it?'

Well, no.

'I'm saying I want a piece of you.'

I think there may have been a growl accompanying that last statement. I didn't stick around to see what nugget he would come up with next.

AGE BEFORE BEAUTY

I'd never used an internet dating site before, but I was sure I'd done all the right things, especially when I found myself chatting to a very eligible 35-year-old man. He was funny and intelligent, and over the next few weeks he charmed me so much that I agreed to meet him – my decision swayed by the photo I'd received of a handsome, craggy-jawed and still young-looking man.

The big day arrived. Being a good girl, I told my mum where I was going to be and when I'd be going there before setting off for the pub car park that we'd agreed to meet in, half-way between our respective homes.

I'd been told to look out for a gentleman in a classic BMW, so I didn't pay much attention to the clapped out banger that parked next to me – nor to the old man who was slowly prising himself out of the front seat. When said man, who I now noticed was wearing a red puffa jacket, clambered over to my car and started tapping on my window and waving, I became confused. Where was my date? And who was this strange man?

Politeness made me stay and have one drink with him after he'd revealed the sad truth to me. Apparently the photo he'd e-mailed to me was over thirty years out of date. He said that he hadn't wanted to tell me that he was actually sixty-seven because I wouldn't have agreed to meet him. He also admitted that he had a grandson who was older than me. But he didn't laugh when I asked for his number instead.

It was an uncomfortable situation. The old chap sat, crotch facing me, digging me now and again with his bony fingers and winking and telling me that he definitely wouldn't need Viagra with someone like me. Meanwhile, the greasy bikers gathered around the bar were spluttering into their pints, not even trying to disguise their amusement at my new friend and me dressed up in my best clothes.

I was just thinking that things couldn't get any worse when I got a text from my brother. 'He looks nice,' it read. 'Bit old for you, don't you reckon, though?' I looked around the pub. Just bikers (still laughing). I got another text: 'Nice jacket he's got, though.' This time when I looked around I saw three heads trying to duck out of sight behind a window. I walked over to see my brother, my mum and my sister sprawled out on the ground outside, tears rolling down their faces. They'd come over to see if I was OK but decided to stay once they'd realized, as they put it, they could 'have a good laugh' at my expense. I got some revenge when I bought them all a drink, introduced them to my horny old friend and then left them there, having to explain where I'd disappeared . . . but that was small compensation for being the laughing stock of the whole village.

ANOTHER OLD STORY

I was invited to a prestigious university ball by a nineteen-year-old gentleman whom I knew through a previous boyfriend. I was then twenty-four myself, and flattered to bits that this young hunk was interested in me. A few minutes after he'd asked me, I made some passing reference that revealed my age – he professed shock and promptly uninvited me, because, he explained, he 'wouldn't want me to feel uncomfortable around all the young people'!

STAGE FRIGHT

I once arranged a date with an actor. He said that he would meet me after a show that he was appearing in at the Almeida Theatre. So after the curtain fell, I stood about hopefully. And then after a while, rather too long a while, instead of just slinking away in silent shame, I asked the theatre staff to search the dressing-rooms for him. Very kindly, they searched there and all over the theatre. And then they put out a message for him on the tannoy.

But he had gone. Worse still, everyone in the building now knew that I had been stood up.

Strangely, I've never gone back to the Almeida since. Still, at least he's never been hugely successful, so I don't see him on telly very much.

WET BLANKET

*I*t was our fifth or sixth date, and I was beginning to wonder if I was falling in love. 'Richard' seemed wonderful. Not quite my type – he looked a bit like he'd stepped out of a perfect-man mould, with his square jaw, wide rugby-playing shoulders, blue eyes and wavy brown hair – but I definitely fancied him, and he was so ideal in other ways that all these physical doubts were rapidly being dispelled. He was a man's man for a start. Tough, macho and strong. He was also witty, charming, attentive and kind. He seemed really earnestly interested in me.

The best thing was that he was also very funny. We'd already got to that happy stage where we felt OK about teasing each other mercilessly, and he could really make me laugh. So much that I almost wet myself a couple of times. Really. He knew all the right buttons to press.

It was during one of these hysterical fits of hilarity that things suddenly went terribly, terribly, God-awfully wrong. We were in his car driving along at a tidy speed on a fast road, guffawing happily. In between chuckles he asked me to pass him a cigarette from inside his coat on the back seat. So, I leaned over and started feeling around in the pocket. The cigarettes seemed to be tangled up in something, which I pulled out too. It was a grey rag, full of holes and slightly damp to the touch.

I waved it at him merrily and asked him what such a *horrible* thing was doing in his pocket.

'What on earth is it?' I wanted to know. 'Ugh!'

For the first time I saw him look uncertain of himself. The smile temporarily left his face, a small cloud passed – but then he was grinning again.

'It's Moopert,' he said.

'What?'

'Moopert. It's my blanket. You know. I've had it for ever. For as long as I can remember anyway.'

I suppose I was looking less than impressed, because he started to look sheepish again.

'I guess I should throw it away really,' he said, 'but . . .'

Suddenly the ultimate tease occurred to me. I would threaten to throw it away! The expression on his face would just be priceless. Barely able to stifle my giggles, I wound down the window and held Moopert up to the wind.

'No!' he screamed, but it was too late. I lost my grip on Moopert when my man slammed on the brakes and I was catapulted towards the front window, only saved from a face full of glass by the seat belt, which I'd fortunately remembered to fasten.

'We've got to find him,' he said as we pulled over into a lay-by, his previous good humour now consumed in anger. 'I don't blame you . . . but . . . but . . .'

All this Moopert business didn't sit well with Richard's macho image, but I'd have been prepared to overlook it, so great was my infatuation. I don't think I'd have been able to forgive what followed, though: two hours in the freezing rain, combing up and down the hedgerows and scrub grass at the side of the road in a vain attempt to find his beloved scrap of blanket while my best date clothes were ruined by the mud and water splashing up from passing vehicles.

However, my own feelings were immaterial, as it turned out. Richard ended things when I finally admitted that I'd seen Moopert getting snagged up in the bonnet of a truck doing 60 m.p.h. up the opposite side of the road, shortly after it had left my hands. He told me that from then on he would have just seen his childhood dying every time he looked into my eyes.

TRIVIA

LOVE HURTS: ROAD KILL

Thirty-two-year-old Kim Fontana and forty-year-old Paul Kowley scooped a 2003 Darwin Award (the annual honours bestowed posthumously on people who stupidly cause their own deaths) for the impromptu – and fatal – shag they had on a Sheffield street. The couple wandered out of a pub, considerably the worse for wear, noticed that a street lamp wasn't working and that the tarmac beneath it was therefore dark – and used said asphalt for some ass-feeling.

Subsequent reports stated that the amorous couple were warned of the dangers of their unusual lovemaking position by three passing drivers.

An off-duty paramedic even told them, 'You want to get up or you'll be run over.'

'Cheers, mate,' Paul replied and blithely carried on getting it on.

Shortly afterwards tragedy struck. The driver of a single-decker bus mistook Paul and Kim for a bag of rubbish lying at the edge of the darkened road and, as one journalist put it, proceeded to press the couple like a pair of trousers. Paramedics found Kim lying on her back with her jumper pulled up, and Paul between her legs with his boxer shorts around his ankles. As the Darwin Award moderators pointed out, the unlucky pair did at least answer the question Paul McCartney posed on The Beatles' *White Album*: 'Why Don't We Do It in the Road?'

IN A SPIN

*M*y big chance to impress the girl I'd been flirting with for months came when she offered to come and pick me up in the brand-new sparkling white car that her rather rich father had just bought her as a reward for passing her driving test.

On mature reflection I can see that my suggestion that she drive me to meet a bunch of my mates in a park in our local town probably wasn't the best one that a would-be Don Juan has ever made. However, I was seventeen, so mature reflection was something I was never going to be able to access. Similarly, I was also completely unable to access the local pubs. My fresh-faced and innocent friends and I were turned away from these with such depressing regularity that the park was the only place we could go to drink beer. And I had to drink beer in order to progress any further with the girl, therefore. . . Well, it made sense at the time, anyway.

Strangely, however, my ability to take the tops off beer bottles with my teeth didn't create a favourable impression on her. Especially since she had to stand soberly by and watch my friends and me get increasingly drunk. No more impressive was the fact that after only two or three of those bottles I was already feeling giddy enough to allow all my other friends to spin me round on a kids' merry-go-round at crazily high speeds. Worse still, the resultant beer and G-forces cocktail ensured that I spent the entire journey home intermittently giggling strangely to myself and then blowing chunks out of the passenger window, leaving red trails of puke all over the new car's white paintwork.

SINGING FOR MY SUPPER

*H*e sang Prince's 'Could You Be the Most Beautiful Girl in the World?' to me. On our first date. In a crowded restaurant. In a terrible, loud voice. And in contrast to His Perfectly Petite Purpleness, my date was more than 6′ 2″ and, erm, quite fat.

Plus, I'm a man. So he had to replace the world 'girl' with 'guy' in every chorus.

Enough said.

TOO CHICKEN

A couple, let's call them John and Joanna – two of my best friends from university – were invited to a party thrown by a mutual friend of ours. This friend had just come back from India, and consequentially there was going to be an Indian theme to the whole affair.

John and Joanna thought it would be nice to invite another couple along on a kind of double date, as this pair vaguely knew the host as well and it would give them someone to talk to in case they didn't know anyone else there.

Come the evening of the party, John – dressed as Apache Indian, famed bangramuffin – and Joanna – got up as Clive of India (though my memory may be deceiving me here) – knocked on the door of the eerily quiet party only to be greeted by the host, dressed perfectly normally.

The horrible realization of the true state of affairs only dawned when they were shown through to the living-room to find a group of people from the subcontinent earnestly tucking into an authentic Indian meal, and looking through the host's photos from her trip. None of them, of course, was in fancy dress.

John and Joanna's extreme embarrassment was then surpassed, however, as the next guests to arrive happened to be the couple they'd invited. They were both dressed as chickens and both wearing T-shirts emblazoned with the words 'Korma' and 'Bhuna' respectively.

PUB LICK HUMILIATION

*M*ost people think working in a pub means you just get chatted up all day and have loads of drinks bought for you. They're wrong. The only contact most men make with barmaids is the one between their eyes and the girls' tits.

Suffice to say, competition was stiff over any nice young men that came to the pub I used to run. I usually bowed out of the contest because of other more pressing issues (such as the Guinness running out), but one particular boy did once catch my attention.

I'm pathologically rubbish at chatting anyone up, but all the girls ganged up and waged a war of attrition on me to pluck up some non-existent courage and talk to him.

I tried. I really, really tried to think of something witty and cool to say that would indicate that I wasn't just any old barmaid, but actually something quite out of the ordinary.

He came to the bar, I gathered myself together, licked my lips and said, 'Do you think you can smell sick?'

FALLING IN LUST

I was a naive yet adventurous teenager spending a year away from the parents, and sexual adventures were naturally at the front of my mind.

During a six-month sojourn on a kibbutz in Israel an opportunity arose that I was not going to let slip. Having admired, only from afar, a beautiful *kibbutznik* for a long time, the evening arrived when, after one vodka too many, I decided to swallow my pride and try my luck on the dance floor.

Unbelievably, she did not take flight when I made my approach and strutted my stuff. Nor did she flinch when I made my move and my arms grasped her close. But when our lips met the room began to spin. Spin around. Faster, and faster. Until I was gripping on to her for dear life. And then it happened . . .

I fell, and I took her with me. In my state I didn't care what everyone around me thought. I had my lady. And I wasn't going to let her go or miss my chance.

When we got up from the floor, I decided there was only one course of action: to ask her back to my room. To my astonishment, she replied in the affirmative.

The walk back was precarious. With the ground tilting at right angles, it would have been easier to crawl . . . and I hit the deck again so many times (doing the gentlemanly thing and this time not taking the lady down with me) that I might just as well have been on all fours.

When we finally made it back to the room, I immediately leaped on to the bed. The lady went to the toilet to powder her nose. In readiness, I unbuckled my trousers and slipped under the covers.

The next thing I knew, I woke up to the sound of a cock crowing. Alone. The lady nowhere to be seen. I remembered nothing, until slowly, so slowly, the memories began to trickle, then flood, back – my one true lust, in my grasp, so cruelly slipped away. Through no one's fault but my own.

I can't entirely blame myself for getting so inebriated. The question remains, however, of whether I would have been able to take such an opportunity if I had not also drunk the quantities that took away all hope I had of catching her . . .

Years on, I ponder it still.

APRÈS PISSED

I travelled out to France by car with three good friends – Big Jon, Dunc and Roland. These three guys were all heavy drinkers, their eagerness to imbibe magnified by the fact that we were going to be there for the New Year.

We got to the hostel and spent the next two days drinking in bars instead of getting out on the slopes. This hadn't been the plan by any means, but the conditions were pretty poor and it was either that or spend Hogmanay in our dormitories at the youth hostel.

I woke up one morning very confused. I looked across the darkened room, waved a rather lame wave to Big Jon, who was clearly still completely pissed, as he was trying to talk to me in German.

I fell back to sleep, and finally came round again wondering (not very hard), why Dunc was in the bed next to me. Dunc also said something in German, which surprised me because, even though he's a worldly chap, I had no idea he was multilingual. I also started to notice, as my eyes continued to rotate in my cranium that Dunc had managed to pull. His prey was lying in the bed next to him. Indeed, our beds were pushed together, and it appeared, or at least started to dawn on me, that all three of us were pretty much in the same bed.

I managed a hazy look over to Big Jon, who appeared to be sat up, but I couldn't properly make out his features, as it was still fairly dark. The curtains were drawn, and it must still have been snowing. However, Big Jon did appear to be slightly smaller than normal, and, oddly, he started talking to me in German again, as if this was our mother tongue and he expected me to understand.

I turned to Dunc and his damsel for help – and it was then that it dawned on me that this man wasn't Dunc at all. Nor was it Jon in the room with me.

It quickly became very clear that I was in my underpants in bed with two unknown Germans, who were slightly bewildered but certainly not hostile. They lay snugly on one side of the pushed-together beds, with me more or less in the other.

As my confusion dawned on them, thankfully, they all started to laugh. They were probably relieved that I'd made a mistake and hadn't tried to get in on any German raunch.

I wasn't in any state of mind to try to explain my way out of the situation, but it gradually became clear to all that I'd got up in the night – probably to go to the loo – and had managed to return to a different dormitory and get into bed with two strangers. They must have taken pity on me, or, more likely, they had been afraid of the big white Y-fronts that I'd been wearing as a joke. (Dunc had received them from his grandma for Christmas.)

I returned to my dorm – which was adorned by various road signs and traffic ornaments. Everyone thought I must have pulled, but the reality was really quite different. It was a very good New Year.

FAILING TO IMPRESS THE LOCALS

*T*he weather in Chamonix had turned far too cold for the preferred T-shirt and sweater, so I had to make a quick visit to a boutique-y snowboard apparel shop to buy a decent jacket for the slopes.

I entered what looked to be a worthy establishment: it had the right logos outside and snowboarding gear in the windows. On entering, to my delight, I saw there were three wonderfully attractive French girl assistants, who didn't appear to be very busy. I smiled inside. Maybe I would be able to impress them. Get to know one, take her to . . .

My daydreams were interrupted by the realization that the three beauties were staring at me. And not in a good way. My scruffy just-got-out-of-bed state dawned on me. I stopped smiling inside. Indeed very quickly the girls' attention began to unnerve me a touch, but I managed to stay composed, nodding politely and making a beeline to the jackets hanging around the store. After a minute or so of checking out the gear the silence in this otherwise empty store and the (probably imagined) sneering started to do my head in. I realized I was breathing quite heavily and was finding it hard to focus on the job in hand. I began fumbling.

I tried a couple of tops on, rather clumsily getting my arms in the wrong sleeves etc. There were little embarrassed glances from all of us and the odd little unnecessary laugh. One assistant, however, then started to look a bit frustrated that I didn't want her help. Another wouldn't look me in the eye, as if I'd offended her too. So much for romance.

At that point I could hold my nerve no longer, and I made my way towards the exit with the apology that nothing really suited – half in French, half in English, but perhaps not making much sense in either language. At least not judging from the girls' blank expressions.

They were all looking at me intently as I walked backwards towards the door. I stepped up the single step to the exit and tripped over it, instantaneously producing from my nose the most enormous 'snot bubble' they had clearly ever seen.

Prior to this monster, I'd no previous experience of such a phenomenon – and I haven't managed to re-create anything resembling it since. It shocked everyone; their faces were the very picture of open-mouthed horror. Yet, not content with my performance so far, and for good measure, I threw in a weedy, squeaky, slightly unhinged 'bonjour' as my withering finale.

TRIVIA

LOVE HURTS: DEAD IMPRESSIVE

Twenty-one-year-old Mexican security guard Victor Alba died instantly when he put his .38 calibre revolver to his head and pulled the trigger. Newspaper *Hoy de La Paz* explained that the unlucky man had been playing Russian roulette 'to impress some female friends'.

A LOAD OF OLD PANTS

*O*ne of my work mates was in Birmingham for a trade show and feeling pretty pleased with himself because he'd managed to entice a girl back to his room. His jubilation turned to horror, however, when it came to the moment to drop his trousers. He suddenly remembered that he'd been unable to find any clean underpants of his own that morning, but since he'd been at his parents', he'd borrowed an old pair from his dad. Unfortunately, not only were these undergarments a good five sizes too big, but they were a rather unique Y-front design from his dad's native Iran . . .

All the same, once the girl had finished laughing at him, they had a good night. So good, in fact, that the next morning she asked for his number. He couldn't find a pen, but he went one better by giving her his business card. What he had forgotten was that, owing to the odd paranoia prevalent in our office about workers giving away their e-mail contact to other would-be employers, the e-mail address on all their business cards just read 'manager@ . . .', and that several people, including our MD, received the messages sent to that address.

So when the girl e-mailed a couple of days later to say thanks for a good night, the whole office got the e-mail. Her message was made even more embarrassing by the fact that she'd told him, 'I still haven't stopped laughing about your pants.'

CALL GIRL

*N*obody was sick. Nobody said anything inappropriate or smelled of something that they shouldn't have smelled of. There wasn't a mix-up involving proximate orifices or identical twins. In fact, nothing happened at all. Nothing. And there's the rub.

I knew her through work. While performing my filing duties, I had managed to convince myself that what I – a graduate with pretensions – really needed was to go on a date with an older woman. A woman with a proper job and a flat. A woman an inventory of whose possessions extended beyond a surfeit of irony, a few paperbacks and an ashtray. A woman with a profession and a place in life. What I needed was a date with one of the criminal lawyers whose papers I was filing.

I just had to convince her. I was surprised by how hard it was. I'd never asked a woman out on a date, so I borrowed a few of the time-honoured approaches that I'd seen working on television. I cornered her in the pub after work on Fridays. I bought her alcohol. I made sure she knew that I found every thought contained in her perfectly shaped head fascinating. And I told her a series of anecdotes, all carefully designed to illustrate how genuine and funny, how misunderstood and sexy, her young colleague was.

In retrospect, my approach was as predictable as an episode of *Columbo*. But I stuck with it, week after week, month after month.

Eventually my persistence paid off. One Friday night, after a few post-work drinks sound-tracked by my self-promoting anecdotes, she decided that we would go to the cinema together the following evening. Yes, she agreed, we should spend more time with each other. She would look at the cinema listings, pick out a film for us to see and a bar for us to meet in. She would phone me at lunchtime the next day to arrange it all. I scribbled out my telephone number for her and went home vindicated and happy.

And what happiness it was. The sense of achievement I felt, having – for the first time – persuaded a *proper woman* to go on a *proper date* was roughly equivalent to passing your driving test and, on arriving back at the test centre, being informed that you'd won a bundle on the Grand National and that you were about to be taken on a victory parade atop the shoulders of your new best friend, Willy Wonka.

It didn't last.

I jumped out of bed at eight o'clock the next morning. I ran out to get a paper. The sun was shining. It was bliss that morning to be alive, but to have a date? Well, that made all the hours of filing worthwhile. I made some coffee, lit a cigarette, opened up the paper to the cinema listings, picked up a book and waited for the all-important call.

My mum called, but I shooed her off the phone – I needed to keep the line clear. Both of my flatmates were away that weekend, which pleased me – I didn't want them giggling or pulling faces while I was organizing my first serious date. But I needn't have worried about that.

At some point in the early afternoon, I ran out of cigarettes. But that was no problem – I told myself that I'd get some after she'd called. By the late afternoon the nicotine cravings were starting to bite, but I couldn't leave the flat because we didn't have an answer-phone. I would wait. I'd seen enough television programmes to know that she'd call the instant I left the flat.

As Saturday afternoon turned into Saturday evening, I found myself walking past the phone quite regularly. I'd find reasons to be near the table in the hallway where it sat. I would glance down at it. Eventually, I decided that I would check to make sure that the line was working. It was, and I should be patient.

A few more hours passed. I dragged the telephone into the living-room so that I could watch it more closely and answer her call more quickly when it came. As the evening passed, I began talking to the phone, imploring it to ring. Gently at first, then more vociferously. I threatened it and bargained with it. I offered it anything it desired. But it didn't ring. It grew dark outside, and still that damned phone didn't ring. Couples passed by on the street outside, perhaps going to the cinema. Telephones in the other flats in my building rang. But not mine. I paced the floor and made tea. We can still make the late show if she calls . . . Now. Or now . . . I turned the lights off and sat in the dark. I turned them all back on again. I listened to *Blood on the Tracks*, but quietly, so that I would be able to hear the call when it came.

By midnight I had become discouraged. And I needed cigarettes. I ran to the all-night shop. On getting back five minutes later, I immediately dialled 1471, fully expecting to have missed her call. To my genuine surprise, I hadn't.

I gave up at 4 a.m. I'd been awake for twenty hours. I needed to rest so that I'd be fresh for the next day. After all, we'd probably got our wires crossed. Maybe we had said Sunday. Yes. We'd go to the cinema, have a drink and laugh about how I'd waited for her call all day, *but on the wrong day*. Perhaps in future this would all be an amusing anecdote – she would ruffle my hair and call me silly. But she would phone tomorrow, and I would wait in, and make sure that I didn't miss her.

Six years on, I've accepted that I'm unlikely to be receiving that call any time soon.

UNTIL DEATH DO US PART

*T*he most exciting one-night stand of my life involved a handsome young man from South Africa. So when my work sent me over there for a conference, I e-mailed him and arranged to spend my last night in the country at his house in Cape Town.

He'd told me that he lived with his parents and grandmother, so I wasn't surprised when I met them all there, but I was a little embarrassed since I didn't know much more about their progeny than the dimensions of the inside of his trousers. Still, I didn't have to talk to them for too long before we were able to make our feeble excuses and head to bed.

I got up earlier than him the morning afterwards, as I had a plane to catch. I wasn't the first up, however. Grandmother was already sitting at the table when I padded into the kitchen to make my coffee. Worryingly, my attempts at small talk were met with cold silence. Did she disapprove of what I'd been doing with her grandson? He'd said she was very understanding – and too old to care much anyway. How odd.

Then I took a closer look at her, and the horrible truth dawned on me. Granny had passed away in the night. She was stone dead.

Appendix 1

ONE-LINERS

The worst chat-up lines at large in the English-speaking world today, as collected on whendatesgobad.co.uk (see page 169).

50. Are you a virgin too?

49. I know what you were thinking, that someone like me would never approach you.

48. Hi! My friends call me Creepy.

47. I think you're really hot. And you've got quite big tits.

46. I may not be the best-looking guy in here, but I'm the only one talking to you.

45. You have the most lovely hair! May I touch you?

44. Is that a false nose?

43. Are you tired? No? Well, you should be. You've been running through my mind all day.

42. My friend wants to know if you think I'm cute.

41. If I was the only man left on earth and was wanted by all women to repopulate the planet, I'd still choose you.

40. Are those real?

39. I've got a great big penis!

38. I have come from the future to tell you that fifty years from now I am still in love with you.

37. Hi, I'm Mr Right. Someone said you were looking for me.

36. Do you sleep on your front? Can I?

35. I'd really like to see how you look when I'm naked.

34. What are you like on all fours howling like a wolf?

33. You know, if I were you, I'd have sex with me.

32. What do I do? I'm studying Marxist theory. [Pause] Would you like to see the Means of Production?

31. Would you like to be buried with my people?

30. Man (says to friend of beautiful woman): Did you want to dance?
    Friend: Oh, yes please.
    Man: Good, because I want to chat up your mate.

29. Oh, I'm sorry, I thought that was a Braille name tag.

28. If a tree falls down in the woods and no one's there, does that mean we should take the opportunity for a bit of al fresco nooky?

27. F@# me if I'm wrong, but is your name Helga Titsbottom?

26. Those clothes would look great in a crumpled heap on my bedroom floor.

25. I wish you were a pony carousel outside Superdrug, so I could ride you all day long for 50p.

24. Is there a mirror in your pants? Because I can see myself in them later.

23. Hello, I think that God would want us to be together.

22. You know what I like in a woman?
    Look slowly and lasciviously down to your own crotch area
    Look back up and raise eyebrow

21. I have had ten fellers. Do you want to make it into a football team?

20. Do you know what virgins eat for breakfast? . . . I thought not!

19. Size isn't everything, and I can prove it to you.

18. Fancy spending a weekend on my 'boat'?

17. Buy me a drink and I'll leave you alone.

16. How do you like your eggs in the morning?

15. Can I buy you a drink, or would you just prefer the money?

14. Your father was a thief . . . He stole all the stars in the sky and put them in your eyes.

13. Your place or mine?

12. Your face or mine?

11. Do you know the difference between my penis and a chicken leg? No? Well, let's go on a picnic and find out!

10. I'm sorry, I was looking for the bathroom, not heaven; could you tell me where the men's room is, angel?

9. Is your dad a terrorist? Because you're da bomb.

8. Do you believe in love at first sight, or should I walk by again?

7. You're the most beautiful girl I've seen on a Wednesday.

6. Hi, my name is Martin. Remember that, because you'll be wanting to scream it at the top of your voice later!

5. You may not be the best-looking girl here, but beauty is only a light switch away.

4. Here's 20p. Go phone your mum and tell her you won't be home tonight.

3. *Licks finger and wipes it on girl's clothes*
   Let's take you home and get you out of those wet things.

2. Do you want to go halves on a bastard?

1. Grab your coat, you've pulled.

The primary motive for collecting and putting up these lines on whendatesgobad.co.uk was that they were so funny – and causing laughter is the only qualification for inclusion in this list. However, some lines cropped up far more often than others, and it seemed like a good idea to tally up their totals and to place those that received the most nominations in the top ten. The Number 1 line has the dubious honour of being the most often nominated.

Appendix 2

DATING DON'TS

Don't be late.

Don't 'forget' your wallet.

Don't forget to turn up.

Don't forget to wash beforehand.

Don't forget to put some clothes on.

Don't forget to talk to the face, not to the breasts.

Don't forget your manners.

Don't argue with the waiter.

Don't insult the waiter.

Don't assault the waiter.

Don't fall in love with the waiter and leave with him instead.

Don't pretend you're something you aren't. Especially if this involves 'special powers'.

Don't talk on your mobile.

Especially don't talk on your mobile to your spouse.

On a first date, don't propose marriage.

On a first date, don't ask how fertile your opposite number is.

Don't ask how many children you think you should have either.

Don't talk about religion.

Don't reveal that you are the Son of God and Saviour of Mankind and that soon ALL will bow before you.

Don't get drunk.

Don't 'liven things up' with a 'little bit' of LSD.

Don't smoke crack in the toilets.

Definitely don't smoke crack in full view of everyone in the restaurant.

Don't fall asleep.

Don't fall over.

Don't come in your pants.

Appendix 3

SHARE YOUR SHAME!

Have you been on a bad date? Have you been stood up or let down? Crushed, humiliated or abused? Great! I'd love to hear about it. Visit www.whendatesgobad.co.uk and tell all.

Or have you been a naughty boy? Or a bad girl? Confess all. You can help assuage your guilt in the cleansing world of web infamy. Or just brag. I'll post the best (and worst!) stories every week – and there are dozens of other new stories of desperation and woe to read there too. I'm still also compiling the list of the most ineffective one-liners in the world. With your help it could become the world's biggest archive of things you really never should say . . .

Acknowledgements

Warm thanks and gratitude to:

Susan Smith, Rowan Yapp, Alex Barker, Jules Ingleby, Dave Russell, Robin Deitch, Lucy Markham, Jon Block, Tim Harcourt, Al Barker, Dan Gibbons, Sorcha Padmore, Chris Jacob, Robin Jones, Martin Shore, Ketan Patel, Lars Hoffman, Nick Bury, Dave Russell, Tom Raleigh, Patrick Raleigh, Adam King, Bronwen Wilson, Fay Miah, Andy Bremner, Becky Hatch, Rosie Scourti, Rob Bailey, Chris Coates, Kevin Mackenzie, Dusty Miller, Jon Butler, Stephen Davison, Mat Wardle, Nick Fisher, Brian McCluskey, Kat Naessens, Laura, Karen, Danielle Kaye, Jo, Sarah Monk, Alison McDougall-Weil and numerous anonymous contributors for stories, support, information and inspiration. Thanks again to Vanessa Baird for providing such a good place to write it in. Jasper Smith, Mat Frankum and Sam the dog at sparks.co.uk for making the website work – and for making the whole process so painless. Terry Kirby, Tahmina Begum at the *London Review of Books*, Damien Weafer at *Private Eye*, the *Gay Times*, popbitch.com, Claie Wilson, Geneviève Roberts, everyone at BBC Radio Oxford, Leslie Anderson and Sinead Desmond for helping to bring in so many fantastic stories. Several of the Beastly Habits trivia sections are adapted from the (highly recommended) *Dr Tatiana's Sex Advice for All Creation*, by Olivia Judson (Chatto and Windus, 2002).